CW00482336

Presented To:

_____

Given By:

_____

A Special Note:

100
PROMISES
AND
PRAYERS
FOR TEENS

Copyright © 2013 by Freeman–Smith, a division of Worthy Media, Inc.

ISBN 978-1-60587-531-6

Published by Freeman-Smith, a division of Worthy Media, Inc.,
134 Franklin Road, Suite 200, Brentwood, Tennessee 37027.

The quoted ideas expressed in this book (but not Scripture verses) are not, in all cases, exact quotations, as some have been edited for clarity and brevity. In all cases, the author has attempted to maintain the speaker's original intent. In some cases, quoted material for this book was obtained from secondary sources, primarily print media. While every effort was made to ensure the accuracy of these sources, the accuracy cannot be guaranteed. For additions, deletions, corrections, or clarifications in future editions of this text, please write Freeman-Smith.

Cover Design by Kim Russell / Wahoo Designs
Page Layout by Bart Dawson

Printed in the United States of America

2 3 4 5—CHG—17 16 15 14 13

100
PROMISES
AND
PRAYERS
FOR TEENS

❋FS

FREEMAN-SMITH

INTRODUCTION

Every life—including yours—is a series of wins and losses, celebrations and disappointments, joys and sorrows. Every step of the way, through every triumph and tragedy, God will stand by your side and strengthen you, if you have faith in Him.

God's promises are eternal and unchanging. But, as every teenager knows, life in today's fast-paced world can be so demanding and so confusing that it's easy to forget God's blessings and His mercy. The ideas on these pages will encourage you to slow down and take inventory of the joys and blessings that God offers to all His children, including you.

This book contains 100 brief devotional readings that are intended to help you strengthen your faith by focusing on God's promises. And make no mistake: God's promises are both eternal and unchanging.

Would you like to build a stronger faith and better future? If so, ask for God's help many times each day, starting with a regular, heartfelt morning devotional. When you do, you will change your day and your life.

READY TO MOVE MOUNTAINS?

For I assure you: If you have faith the size of a mustard seed, you will tell this mountain, "Move from here to there," and it will move. Nothing will be impossible for you.
Matthew 17:20 HCSB

Because we live in a demanding world, all of us have mountains to climb and mountains to move. Moving those mountains requires faith.

Are you a mountain-moving Christian whose faith is evident for all to see? Or, are you a spiritual underachiever? As you think about the answer to that question, consider this: God needs more people who are willing to move mountains for His glory and for His kingdom.

Are you willing to let God help you move mountains, or are you still stumbling around over a few little molehills? The answer should be obvious. And so, with no more delays, let the mountain moving begin.

Faith is stronger than fear.

John Maxwell

Faith never knows where it is being led, but it loves and knows the One Who is leading.

Oswald Chambers

Great hopes make great men.

Thomas Fuller

We are never stronger than the moment we admit we are weak.

Beth Moore

TODAY'S PRAYER

Dear Lord, help me strengthen my faith—and share it—today and every day of my life. Amen

CHOOSING TO BEAR WITNESS TO GOD'S TRUTH

You will know the truth,
and the truth will set you free.
John 8:32 HCSB

God is vitally concerned with truth. His Word teaches the truth; His Spirit reveals the truth; His Son leads us to the truth. When we open our hearts to God, and when we allow His Son to rule over our thoughts and our lives, God reveals Himself, and we come to understand the truth about ourselves and the Truth (with a capital T) about God's gift of grace.

The familiar words of John 8:32 remind us that when we come to know God's Truth, we are liberated. Have you been liberated by that Truth? And are you living in accordance with the eternal truths that you find in God's Holy Word? Hopefully so.

Today, as you fulfill the responsibilities that God has placed before you, ask yourself this question: "Do my thoughts and actions bear witness to the ultimate Truth that God has placed in my heart, or am I allowing the pressures of everyday life to overwhelm me?" It's a profound question that deserves an answer . . . now.

We must go out and live among them, manifesting the gentle, loving spirit of our Lord. We need to make friends before we can hope to make converts.

Lottie Moon

TODAY'S PRAYER

Heavenly Father, You are the way and the truth and the light. Today—as I follow Your way and share Your Good News—let me be a worthy example to others and a worthy servant to You. Amen

HE'S HERE

I am not alone, because the Father is with Me.
John 16:32 HCSB

Do you ever wonder if God really hears your prayers? If so, you're in good company: lots of very faithful Christians have wondered the same thing. In fact, some of the biggest heroes in the Bible had their doubts—and so, perhaps, will you. But when you have your doubts, remember this: God isn't on vacation, and He hasn't moved out of town. God isn't taking a coffee break, and He isn't snoozing on the couch. He's right here, right now, listening to your thoughts and prayers, watching over your every move.

As the demands of everyday life weigh down upon you, you may be tempted to ignore God's presence or—worse yet—to rebel against His commandments. But, when you quiet yourself and acknowledge His presence, God touches your heart and restores your spirits. So why not let Him do it right now?

Get yourself into the presence of the loving Father. Just place yourself before Him, and look up into, His face; think of His love, His wonderful, tender, pitying love.

Andrew Murray

Our battles are first won or lost in the secret places of our will in God's presence, never in full view of the world.

Oswald Chambers

God walks with us. He scoops us up in His arms or simply sits with us in silent strength until we cannot avoid the awesome recognition that yes, even now, He is here.

Gloria Gaither

TODAY'S PRAYER

Dear Lord, You are always near. Yet I sometimes feel so far from You. During those times, help me sense Your presence . . . and Your love. Amen

13

WHO RULES YOUR HEART?

For God so loved the world that he gave his one and only Son, that whoever believes in him shall not perish but have eternal life.

John 3:16 NIV

Your decision to allow Christ to reign over your heart is the pivotal decision of your life. It is a decision that you cannot ignore. It is a decision that is yours and yours alone.

God's love for you is deeper and more profound than you can imagine. God's love for you is so great that He sent His only Son to this earth to die for your sins and to offer you the priceless gift of eternal life. Now, you must decide whether or not to accept God's gift. Will you ignore it or embrace it? Will you accept Christ's love and build a lifelong relationship with Him, or will you turn away from Him and take a different path?

Accept God's gift now: allow His Son to preside over your heart, your thoughts, and your life, starting this very instant.

Evidence of new birth is that we see the rule of God.

Oswald Chambers

The amount of power you experience to live a victorious, triumphant Christian life is directly proportional to the freedom you give the Spirit to be Lord of your life!

Anne Graham Lotz

Choose Jesus Christ! Deny yourself, take up the Cross, and follow Him—for the world must be shown. The world must see, in us, a discernible, visible, startling difference.

Elisabeth Elliot

TODAY'S PRAYER

Father, You sent Your Son that I might have life eternal. Thank You for this priceless gift and for the joy I feel in my heart when I give You my thoughts, my prayers, my praise, and my life. Amen

QUESTIONS, QUESTIONS, QUESTIONS

Now if any of you lacks wisdom, he should ask God, who gives to all generously and without criticizing, and it will be given to him. But let him ask in faith without doubting. For the doubter is like the surging sea, driven and tossed by the wind.

James 1:5-6 HCSB

So many questions and so few answers! If that statement seems to describe the current state of your spiritual life, don't panic. Even the most faithful Christians are overcome by occasional bouts of fear and doubt. You are no different.

When you feel that your faith is being tested to its limits, seek the comfort and assurance of the One who sent His Son as a sacrifice for you. And remember: Even when you feel very distant from God, God is never distant from you. When you sincerely seek His presence, He will touch your heart, calm your fears, and restore your soul.

When there is perplexity there is always guidance—not always at the moment we ask, but in good time, which is God's time. There is no need to fret and stew.

Elisabeth Elliot

We are finding we don't have such a gnawing need to know the answers when we know the Answer.

Gloria Gaither

Be to the world a sign that while we as Christians do not have all the answers, we do know and care about the questions.

Billy Graham

TODAY'S PRAYER

Dear Lord, when I have questions that I can't answer, I will trust You. And I will do my best to offer help to those who need it, so that through me, others, too, might come to know You and trust You. Amen

GOD CAN HANDLE IT

*Give your burdens to the Lord,
and he will take care of you.
He will not permit the godly to slip and fall.*
Psalm 55:22 NLT

It's a promise that is made over and over again in the Bible: Whatever "it" is, God can handle it.

Life isn't always easy. Far from it! Sometimes, life can be very, very tough. But even then, even during our darkest moments, we're protected by a loving Heavenly Father. When we're worried, God can reassure us; when we're sad, God can comfort us. When our hearts are broken, God is not just near, He is here. So we must lift our thoughts and prayers to Him. When we do, He will answer our prayers. Why? Because He is our Shepherd, and He has promised to protect us now and forever.

You may not know what you are going to do; you only know that God knows what He is going to do.

Oswald Chambers

The next time you're disappointed, don't panic. Don't give up. Just be patient and let God remind you he's still in control.

Max Lucado

Your greatest ministry will likely come out of your greatest hurt.

Rick Warren

TODAY'S PRAYER

Lord, sometimes life is so difficult that I can't see any hope for the future. But with You, there is always hope. Keep me mindful that there is nothing that will happen today that You and I can't handle together. Amen

A BOOK UNLIKE ANY OTHER

*For I am not ashamed of the gospel,
because it is God's power for salvation
to everyone who believes.*
Romans 1:16 HCSB

The Bible can be a powerful tool for strengthening our faith. George Mueller observed, "The vigor of our spiritual lives will be in exact proportion to the place held by the Bible in our lives and in our thoughts." As Christians, we are called upon to study God's Holy Word and then apply it to our lives. When we do, we are blessed.

The Bible is a priceless gift, a tool for Christians to use as they share the Good News of their Savior, Christ Jesus. Too many Christians, however, keep their spiritual tool kits tightly closed and out of sight. God's Holy Word is, indeed, a priceless, one-of-a-kind treasure. Handle it with care, but, more importantly, handle it every day.

Nobody ever outgrows Scripture; the book widens and deepens with our years.

C. H. Spurgeon

God gives us a compass and a Book of promises and principles—the Bible—and lets us make our decisions day by day as we sense the leading of His Spirit. This is how we grow.

Warren Wiersbe

The Bible is the one Book to which any thoughtful man may go with any honest question of life or destiny and find the answer of God by honest searching.

John Ruskin

TODAY'S PRAYER

Dear Lord, the Bible is Your gift to me. I will use it, I will trust it, and I will obey it, today and every day that I live. Amen

ASK GOD FOR HELP

*And yet the reason you don't have
what you want is that you don't ask God for it.*
James 4:2 HCSB

Sometimes, amid the stresses and the frustrations of daily life, we forget to slow ourselves down long enough to talk with God. Instead of turning our thoughts and prayers to Him, we rely entirely upon our own resources, with decidedly mixed results. Or, instead of praying for strength, we seek to manufacture it within ourselves, only to find that lasting strength remains elusive.

Are you in need? Ask God to sustain you. And while you're in the mood to ask, don't be afraid to ask for the loving support of your family and friends. When you ask for help, you're likely to receive it. But if you're unwilling to ask, why should you expect to receive it?

So the next time times get tough, remember that help is on the way . . . all you must do is ask.

God will help us become the people we are meant to be, if only we will ask Him.

Hannah Whitall Smith

When trials come your way—as inevitably they will—do not run away. Run to your God and Father.

Kay Arthur

Often I have made a request of God with earnest pleadings even backed up with Scripture, only to have Him say "No" because He had something better in store.

Ruth Bell Graham

TODAY'S PRAYER

Lord, when I have questions or fears, let me turn to You. When I am weak, let me seek Your strength. When I am discouraged, Father, keep me mindful of Your love and Your grace. In all things, let me seek Your will and Your way, Dear Lord, today and forever. Amen

LOOK FOR MIRACLES

*God verified the message by signs and wonders
and various miracles and by giving gifts
of the Holy Spirit whenever he chose to do so.*

Hebrews 2:4 NLT

One way we can strengthen our faith is by looking carefully at the miraculous things that God does. But sometimes, we're simply too preoccupied to notice. Instead of paying careful attention to God's handiwork, we become distracted. Instead of expecting God to work miracles, we become cynical. Instead of depending on God's awesome power, we seek to muddle along using our own power—with decidedly mixed results.

Miracles, both great and small, are an integral part of everyday life—and they are a part of your life, too. But here's the million-dollar question: have you noticed?

If you lack the faith that God can work miracles in your own life, it's time to reconsider. Instead of doubting God, trust His power, and expect His miracles.

Only God can move mountains, but faith and prayer can move God.

E. M. Bounds

When God is involved, anything can happen. Be open and stay that way. God has a beautiful way of bringing good vibrations out of broken chords.

Charles Swindoll

I could go through this day oblivious to the miracles all around me or I could tune in and "enjoy."

Gloria Gaither

TODAY'S PRAYER

Lord, for You, nothing is impossible. Let me trust in Your power to do the miraculous, and let me trust in Your willingness to work miracles in my life—and in my heart. Amen

25

ENTRUSTING YOUR HOPES TO GOD

You, Lord, give true peace to those who depend on you, because they trust you.

Isaiah 26:3 NCV

There are few sadder sights on earth than the sight of a girl or guy who has lost hope. In difficult times, hope can be elusive, but those who place their faith in God's promises need never lose it. After all, God is good; His love endures; He has promised His children the gift of eternal life. And, God keeps His promises.

If you find yourself falling into the spiritual traps of worry and discouragement, seek the healing touch of Jesus and the encouraging words of fellow believers. And if you find a friend in need, remind him or her of the peace that is found through a genuine relationship with Christ. It was Christ who promised, "I have told you these things so that in Me you may have peace. In the world you have suffering. But take courage! I have conquered the world" (John 16:33 HCSB). This world can be a place of trials and troubles, but as believers, we are secure. God has promised us peace, joy, and eternal life. And, of course, God keeps His promises today, tomorrow, and forever.

Hope is faith holding out its hand in the dark.

Barbara Johnson

The will of God is the most delicious and delightful thing in the universe.

Hannah Whitall Smith

TODAY'S PRAYER

Dear Lord, make me a hope-filled Christian. If I become discouraged, let me turn to You. If I grow tired, let me seek strength in You. In every aspect of my life, I will trust You, Father, today and forever. Amen

CELEBRATE LIFE

This is the day the Lord has made;
let us rejoice and be glad in it.
Psalm 118:24 HCSB

Do you want to know God more intimately? Try this: celebrate the life He has given you.

Do you feel like celebrating today? If you're a believer, you should. When you allow Christ to reign over your heart, today and every day should be a time for joyful celebration.

What do you expect from the day ahead? Are you expecting God to do wonderful things, or are you living beneath a cloud of worry and doubt? The words of Psalm 118:24 remind us that every day is a gift from God. So whatever this day holds for you, begin it and end it with God as your partner and Christ as your Savior. And through-out the day, give thanks to the One who created you and saved you. God's love for you is infinite. Accept it; celebrate it; and be thankful.

Some of us seem so anxious about avoiding hell that we forget to celebrate our journey toward heaven.

Philip Yancey

If you can forgive the person you were, accept the person you are, and believe in the person you will become, you are headed for joy. So celebrate your life.

Barbara Johnson

Unparalleled joy and victory come from allowing Christ to do "the hard thing" with us.

Beth Moore

TODAY'S PRAYER

Dear Lord, You have given me so many blessings, too many to count. I will celebrate the life You have given me. And, I will share my joy with my family, with my friends, and with my neighbors, this day and every day. Amen

GOD DOESN'T CHANGE

For I am the Lord, I do not change.
Malachi 3:6 NKJV

We live in a world that is always changing, but we worship the God who never changes—thank goodness! That means that we can be comforted in the knowledge that our Heavenly Father is the rock that simply cannot be moved: "I am the Lord, I do not change" (Malachi 3:6 NKJV).

The next time you face difficult circumstances, tough times, unfair treatment, or unwelcome changes, remember that some things never change—things like the love that you feel in your heart for your family and friends . . . and the love that God feels for you. So, instead of worrying too much about life's inevitable challenges, focus your energies on finding solutions. Have faith in your own abilities, do your best to solve your problems, and leave the rest up to God.

The secret of contentment in the midst of change is found in having roots in the changeless Christ—the same yesterday, today and forever.

Ed Young

The resurrection of Jesus Christ is the power of God to change history and to change lives.

Bill Bright

Conditions are always changing; therefore, I must not be dependent upon conditions. What matters supremely is my soul and my relationship to God.

Corrie ten Boom

TODAY'S PRAYER

Dear Lord, our world is constantly changing. When I face the inevitable transitions of life, I will turn to You for strength and assurance. Thank You, Father, for love that is unchanging and everlasting. Amen

A WALK WITH GOD

In all things showing yourself to be a pattern of good works, in doctrine showing integrity, reverence, incorruptibility . . . .

Titus 2:7 NKJV

Beth Moore correctly observed, "Those who walk in truth walk in liberty." Godly guys and girls agree. As believers in Christ, we must seek to live each day with discipline, honesty, and faith. When we do, at least two things happen: integrity becomes a habit, and God blesses us because of our obedience to Him. Living a life of integrity isn't always the easiest way, but in the long run, it's the more peaceful—and less stressful—way to live.

Character isn't built overnight; it is built slowly over a lifetime. It is the sum of every sensible choice, every honorable decision, and every honest word. It is forged on the anvil of sincerity and polished by the virtue of fairness. Character is a precious thing—preserve yours at all costs.

Integrity is the glue that holds our way of life together. We must constantly strive to keep our integrity intact. When wealth is lost, nothing is lost; when health is lost, something is lost; when character is lost, all is lost.

Billy Graham

No man can use his Bible with power unless he has the character of Jesus in his heart.

Alan Redpath

The man who cannot believe in himself cannot believe in anything else. The basis of all integrity and character is whatever faith we have in our own integrity.

Roy L. Smith

TODAY'S PRAYER

Heavenly Father, help me see the truth, help me speak the truth, and help me live the truth—today and every day of my life. Amen

33

RICHLY BLESSED

The Lord bless you and keep you;
The Lord make His face shine upon you,
And be gracious to you.
Numbers 6:24-25 NKJV

Have you counted your blessings lately? If you sincerely wish to follow in Christ's footsteps, you should make thanksgiving a habit, a regular part of your daily routine.

How has God blessed you? First and foremost, He has given you the gift of eternal life through the sacrifice of His only begotten Son, but the blessings don't stop there. Today, take time to make a partial list of God's gifts to you: the talents, the opportunities, the possessions, and the relationships that you may, on occasion, take for granted. And then, when you've spent sufficient time listing your blessings, offer a prayer of gratitude to the Giver of all things good . . . and, to the best of your ability, use your gifts for the glory of His kingdom.

It is when we give ourselves to be a blessing that we can specially count on the blessing of God.

Andrew Murray

We prevent God from giving us the great spiritual gifts He has in store for us, because we do not give thanks for daily gifts.

Dietrich Bonhoeffer

God's kindness is not like the sunset—brilliant in its intensity, but dying every second. God's generosity keeps coming and coming and coming.

Bill Hybels

TODAY'S PRAYER

Lord, I have more blessings than I can possibly count; make me mindful of Your precious gifts. I will give thanks and praise You always. Today, let me share Your blessings with others, just as You first shared them with me. Amen

A SERIES OF CHOICES

*But the wisdom from above is first pure,
then peace-loving, gentle, compliant, full of mercy
and good fruits, without favoritism and hypocrisy.*
James 3:17 HCSB

Your life is a series of choices. From the instant you wake up in the morning until the moment you nod off to sleep at night, you make countless decisions—decisions about the things you do, decisions about the words you speak, and decisions about the way that you choose to direct your thoughts.

As a believer who has been transformed by the love of Jesus, you have every reason to make wise choices. But sometimes, when the stresses of the daily grind threaten to grind you up and spit you out, you may make choices that are displeasing to God. When you do, you'll pay a price because you'll forfeit the happiness and the peace that might otherwise have been yours.

So, as you pause to consider the kind of Christian you are—and the kind of Christian you want to become—ask yourself whether you're sitting on the fence or standing in the light. The choice is yours . . . and so are the consequences.

The greatest choice any man makes is to let God choose for him.

Vance Havner

Every day, I find countless opportunities to decide whether I will obey God and demonstrate my love for Him or try to please myself or the world system. God is waiting for my choices.

Bill Bright

TODAY'S PRAYER

Lord, help me to make choices that are pleasing to You. Help me to be honest, patient, and kind. And above all, help me to follow the teachings of Jesus, not just today, but every day. Amen

37

BE A COURAGEOUS CHRISTIAN

Be strong and courageous, and do the work.
Don't be afraid or discouraged,
for the Lord God, my God, is with you.
He won't leave you or forsake you.

1 Chronicles 28:20 HCSB

Because we are saved by a risen Christ, we can have hope for the future, no matter how desperate our circumstances may seem. After all, God has promised that we are His throughout eternity. And, He has told us that we must place our hopes in Him.

Today, summon the courage to follow God. Even if the path seems difficult, even if your heart is fearful, trust your Heavenly Father and follow Him. Trust Him with your day and your life. Do His work, care for His children, and share His Good News. Let Him guide your steps. He will not lead you astray.

Choose Jesus Christ! Deny yourself, take up the Cross, and follow Him—for the world must be shown. The world must see, in us, a discernible, visible, startling difference.

Elisabeth Elliot

Be careful how you live. You may be the only Bible some person ever reads.

William J. Toms

The central Christian belief is that Christ's death has somehow put us right with God and given us a fresh start.

C. S. Lewis

TODAY'S PRAYER

Dear Lord, help me to be a practical Christian, a person who's quick to respond to the needs I see around me. Give me the strength, the vision, and the wisdom to put my faith into action today, tomorrow, and every day of my life. Amen

39

DON'T OVERESTIMATE THE IMPORTANCE OF APPEARANCES

As the water reflects the face,
so the heart reflects the person.
Proverbs 27:19 HCSB

The world sees you as you appear to be; God sees you as you really are. He sees your heart, and He understands your intentions. The opinions of others should be relatively unimportant to you; however, God's view of you—His understanding of your actions, your thoughts, and your motivations—should be vitally important.

Few things in life are more futile than "keeping up appearances" in order to impress your friends and your dates—yet the media would have you believe otherwise. The media would have you believe that everything depends on the color of your hair, the condition of your wardrobe, and the model of the car you drive. But nothing could be further from the truth. What is important, of course, is pleasing your Father in heaven. You please Him when your intentions are pure and your actions are just. When you do, you will be blessed today, tomorrow, and forever.

Outside appearances, things like the clothes you wear or the car you drive, are important to other people but totally unimportant to God. Trust God.

Marie T. Freeman

TODAY'S PRAYER

Dear Lord, the world focuses on my outward appearance, but You see my heart. Today, Father, I will guard my heart as I focus, not upon outward appearances, but upon the real person I am today, and the person I can become tomorrow. Amen

DISCIPLINE NOW

*But I discipline my body and bring it into subjection,
lest, when I have preached to others,
I myself should become disqualified.*
1 Corinthians 9:27 NKJV

God doesn't reward laziness, misbehavior, or apathy. To the contrary, He expects His followers to behave with dignity and discipline. But sometimes, it's extremely difficult to be dignified and disciplined. Why? Because the world wants us to believe that dignified, self-disciplined behavior is going out of style.

Face facts: Life's greatest rewards aren't likely to fall into your lap. To the contrary, your greatest accomplishments will probably require lots of work, which is perfectly fine with God. After all, He knows that you're up to the task, and He has big plans for you. God will do His part to fulfill those plans, and the rest, of course, is up to you.

Personal humility is a spiritual discipline and the hallmark of the service of Jesus.

Franklin Graham

The alternative to discipline is disaster.

Vance Havner

As we seek to become disciples of Jesus Christ, we should never forget that the word disciple is directly related to the word discipline. To be a disciple of the Lord Jesus Christ is to know his discipline.

Dennis Swanberg

TODAY'S PRAYER

Lord, I want to be a disciplined believer. Let me use my time wisely, and let me teach others by the faithfulness of my conduct, today and every day. Amen

WHEN THE PATH IS DARK

Though I sit in darkness, the Lord will be my light.
Micah 7:8 HCSB

Doubts come in several shapes and sizes: doubts about God, doubts about the future, and doubts about our own abilities, for starters. But when doubts creep in, as they will from time to time, we need not despair. As Sheila Walsh observed, "To wrestle with God does not mean that we have lost faith, but that we are fighting for it."

God never leaves our side, not for an instant. He is always with us, always willing to calm the storms of life. When we sincerely seek His presence—and when we genuinely seek to establish a deeper, more meaningful relationship Him—God is prepared to touch our hearts, to calm our fears, to answer our doubts, and to restore our confidence.

Mark it down. God never turns away the honest seeker. Go to God with your questions. You may not find all the answers, but in finding God, you know the One who does.

Max Lucado

Doubting may temporarily disturb, but will not permanently destroy, your faith in Christ.

Charles Swindoll

Feelings of uselessness and hopelessness are not from God, but from the evil one, the devil, who wants to discourage you and thwart your effectiveness for the Lord.

Bill Bright

TODAY'S PRAYER

Dear Lord, when I am filled with uncertainty and doubt, give me faith. In the dark moments of life, keep me mindful of Your healing power and Your infinite love, so that I may live courageously and faithfully today and every day. Amen

TODAY IS A NEW BEGINNING

You are being renewed in the spirit of your minds;
you put on the new man, the one created
according to God's likeness in righteousness
and purity of the truth.
Ephesians 4:23-24 HCSB

Each new day offers countless opportunities to serve God, to seek His will, and to obey His teachings. But each day also offers countless opportunities to stray from God's commandments.

Sometimes, we wander aimlessly in a wilderness of our own making, but God has better plans for us. And, whenever we ask Him to renew our strength and guide our steps, He does so.

Consider this day a new beginning. Consider it a fresh start, a renewed opportunity to serve your Creator with willing hands and a loving heart. Ask God to renew your sense of purpose as He guides your steps. Today is a glorious opportunity to serve God. Seize that opportunity while you can; tomorrow may indeed be too late.

No matter how badly we have failed, we can always get up and begin again. Our God is the God of new beginnings.

Warren Wiersbe

Sometimes your medicine bottle has on it, "Shake well before using." That is what God has to do with some of His people. He has to shake them well before they are ever usable.

Vance Havner

More often than not, when something looks like it's the absolute end, it is really the beginning.

Charles Swindoll

TODAY'S PRAYER

O Lord, create in me a clean heart, a new heart that reflects Your love for me. When I need to change, change me, Lord, and make me new. Amen

STAND UP
FOR YOUR BELIEFS

I know whom I have believed and am
persuaded that He is able to guard what has been
entrusted to me until that day.

2 Timothy 1:12 HCSB

In describing one's beliefs, actions are far better descriptors than words. Yet far too many of us spend more energy talking about our beliefs than living by them—with predictable consequences.

Is your life a picture book of your creed? Are your actions congruent with your beliefs? Are you willing to practice the philosophy that you preach? If so, you'll most certainly feel better about yourself.

Today, make certain that your actions are guided by God's Word and by the conscience that He has placed in your heart. Don't treat your faith as if it were separate from your everyday life. Weave your beliefs into the very fabric of your day. When you do, God will honor your good works, and your good works will honor God.

Belief is not the result of an intellectual act; it is the result of an act of my will whereby I deliberately commit myself.

Oswald Chambers

You may as well quit reading and hearing the Word of God and give it to the devil if you do not desire to live according to it.

Martin Luther

God's presence is with you, but you have to make a choice to believe—and I mean, really believe—that this is true. This conscious decision is yours alone.

Bill Hybels

TODAY'S PRAYER

Heavenly Father, I believe in You, and I believe in Your Word. Help me to live in such a way that my actions validate my beliefs—and let the glory be Yours forever. Amen

FULLY GROWN?

*So let us stop going over the basics of Christianity
again and again. Let us go on instead
and become mature in our understanding.*

Hebrews 6:1 NLT

Are you about as mature as you're ever going to be? Hopefully not! When it comes to your faith, God doesn't intend for you to become "fully grown," at least not in this lifetime.

As a Christian, you should continue to grow in the love and the knowledge of your Savior as long as you live. How? By studying God's Word, by obeying His commandments, and by allowing His Son to reign over your heart.

Are you continually seeking to become a more mature believer? Hopefully so, because that's exactly what you owe to God and to yourself.

A person who gazes and keeps on gazing at Jesus becomes like him in appearance.

E. Stanley Jones

The Scriptures were not given for our information, but for our transformation.

D. L. Moody

Be filled with the Holy Spirit; join a church where the members believe the Bible and know the Lord; seek the fellowship of other Christians; learn and be nourished by God's Word and His many promises. Conversion is not the end of your journey—it is only the beginning.

Corrie ten Boom

TODAY'S PRAYER

Lord, help me to keep growing spiritually and emotionally. Let me live according to Your Word, and let me grow in my faith every day that I live. Amen

REMEMBER CHRIST'S LOVE

*For I am persuaded that neither death nor life,
nor angels nor rulers, nor things present, nor things
to come, nor powers, nor height, nor depth,
nor any other created thing will have the power
to separate us from the love of God
that is in Christ Jesus our Lord!*

Romans 8:38-39 HCSB

How much does Christ love us? More than we, as mere mortals, can comprehend. His love is perfect and steadfast. Even though we are imperfect and wayward, the Good Shepherd cares for us still. Even though we have fallen far short of the Father's commandments, Christ loves us with a power and depth that are beyond our understanding. The sacrifice that Jesus made upon the cross was made for each of us, and His love endures to the edge of eternity and beyond.

Christ's love changes everything, including your relationships. When you accept His gift of grace, you are transformed, not only for today, but also for all eternity.

Jesus is waiting patiently for you to invite Him into your heart. Please don't make Him wait a single minute longer.

He loved us not because we're lovable, but because He is love.

C. S. Lewis

God is my heavenly Father. He loves me with an everlasting love. The proof of that is the Cross.

Elisabeth Elliot

TODAY'S PRAYER

Dear Jesus, I praise You for Your love, a love that never ends. Today, I will return Your love and I will share it with the world. Amen

GET INVOLVED
IN A CHURCH

For where two or three come together in my name,
there am I with them.

Matthew 18:20 NIV

A good way to figure out the kind of person you want to become is by worshiping with people who love and respect you. That's one reason (but certainly not the only reason) that you should be an active member of a supportive congregation.

Every believer—including you—needs to be part of a community of faith. Your association with fellow Christians should be uplifting, enlightening, encouraging, and consistent.

Are you an active member of your fellowship? Are you a builder of bridges inside the four walls of your church and outside it? Do you contribute your time and your talents to a close-knit band of hope-filled believers? Hopefully so. The fellowship of believers is intended to be a powerful tool for spreading God's Good News and uplifting His children. God intends for you to be a fully contributing member of that fellowship. Your intentions should be the same.

_____

The church has no greater need today than to fall in love with Jesus all over again.

Vance Havner

Only participation in the full life of a local church builds spiritual muscle.

Rick Warren

The Bible knows nothing of solitary religion.

John Wesley

TODAY'S PRAYER

Heavenly Father, I give thanks for my church and for the opportunity to worship there. Guide my steps, Lord, as I worship You in spirit and in truth, today and forever. Amen

LISTEN CAREFULLY TO YOUR CONSCIENCE

Now the goal of our instruction is love from a pure heart, a good conscience, and a sincere faith.
1 Timothy 1:5 HCSB

Billy Graham correctly observed, "Most of us follow our conscience as we follow a wheelbarrow. We push it in front of us in the direction we want to go." To do so, of course, is a profound mistake. Yet all of us, on occasion, have failed to listen to the voice that God planted in our hearts, and all of us have suffered the consequences.

God gave you a conscience for a very good reason: to make your path conform to His will. Wise believers make it a practice to listen carefully to that quiet internal voice. Count yourself among that number. When your conscience speaks, listen and learn. In all likelihood, God is trying to get His message through. And in all likelihood, it is a message that you desperately need to hear.

To go against one's conscience is neither safe nor right. Here I stand. I cannot do otherwise.

Martin Luther

The convicting work of the Holy Spirit awakens, disturbs, and judges.

Franklin Graham

God desires that we become spiritually healthy enough through faith to have a conscience that rightly interprets the work of the Holy Spirit.

Beth Moore

TODAY'S PRAYER

Dear Lord, today, I will honor the quiet voice that You have placed in my heart. I will strive to obey Your Word as I follow in the footsteps of Your Son today, tomorrow, and every day of my life. Amen

LOOK FOR FULFILLMENT IN ALL THE RIGHT PLACES

Until now you have not asked for anything
in my name. Ask and you will receive,
so that your joy will be the fullest possible joy.
John 16:24 NCV

Where can we find fulfillment and content-ment? Is it a result of wealth, or power, or beauty, or fame? Hardly. Genuine contentment is a gift from God to those who trust Him and follow His commandments.

Our modern world seems preoccupied with the search for happiness. We are bombarded with messages telling us that happiness depends upon the acquisition of material possessions. These messages are false. Enduring peace is not the re-sult of our acquisitions; it is a spiritual gift from God to those who obey Him and accept His will. If we don't find contentment in God, we will never find it anywhere else. But, if we seek Him and obey Him, we will be blessed with an inner peace that is beyond human understanding. When God dwells at the center of our lives, peace and contentment will belong to us just as surely as we belong to God.

We are never more fulfilled than when our longing for God is met by His presence in our lives.

Billy Graham

We will never be happy until we make God the source of our fulfillment and the answer to our longings.

Stormie Omartian

TODAY'S PRAYER

Dear Lord, You offer me contentment and peace; let me accept Your peace. Help me to trust Your Word, to follow Your commandments, and to welcome the peace of Jesus into my heart, today and forever. Amen

59

THE IMPORTANCE OF COURTESY

Be hospitable to one another without grumbling.
1 Peter 4:9 NKJV

Did Christ instruct us in matters of etiquette and courtesy? Of course He did. Christ's instructions are clear: "In everything, therefore, treat people the same way you want them to treat you, for this is the Law and the Prophets" (Matthew 7:12 NASB). Jesus did not say, "In some things, treat people as you wish to be treated." And, He did not say, "From time to time, treat others with kindness." Christ said that we should treat others as we wish to be treated in every aspect of our daily lives. This is a tall order indeed, but as Christians, we are commanded to do our best.

Today, be a little kinder than necessary to family members, friends, and total strangers. And, as you consider all the things that Christ has done in your life, honor Him with your words and with your deeds.

When you extend hospitality to others, you're not trying to impress people; you're trying to reflect God to them.

Max Lucado

Only the courteous can love, but it is love that makes them courteous.

C. S. Lewis

If you are willing to honor a person out of respect for God, you can be assured that God will honor you.

Beth Moore

TODAY'S PRAYER

Guide me, Lord, to treat all those I meet with courtesy and respect. You have created each person in Your own image; let me honor those who cross my path with the dignity that You have bestowed upon them. We are all Your children, Lord; let me show kindness to all. Amen

SAYING YES TO GOD

*Cast your burden upon the Lord
and He will sustain you: He will never allow
the righteous to be shaken.*

Psalm 55:22 NASB

Your decision to seek a deeper relationship with God will not remove all problems from your life; to the contrary, it will bring about a series of personal crises as you constantly seek to say "yes" to God, although the world encourages you to do otherwise. You live in a world that seeks to snare your attention and lead you away from God. Each time you are tempted to distance yourself from the Creator, you will face a spiritual crisis. A few of these crises may be monumental in scope, but most will be the small, everyday decisions of life. In fact, life can be seen as one test after another—and with each crisis comes yet another opportunity to grow closer to God.

Today, you will face many opportunities to say "yes" to your Creator—and you will also encounter many opportunities to say "no" to Him. Your answers will determine the quality of your day and the direction of your life, so answer carefully . . . very carefully.

We all go through pain and sorrow, but the presence of God, like a warm, comforting blanket, can shield us and protect us, and allow the deep inner joy to surface, even in the most devastating circumstances.

Barbara Johnson

Our heavenly Father never takes anything from his children unless he means to give them something better.

George Mueller

TODAY'S PRAYER

Dear God, when I'm having a bad day, help me remember that troubles are temporary, but Your love lasts forever. Amen

MEET WITH GOD EVERY MORNING

Morning by morning he wakens me and opens my understanding to his will. The Sovereign Lord has spoken to me, and I have listened.

Isaiah 50:4-5 NLT

Want to strengthen your faith? Then schedule a meeting with God every day.

Daily life is a tapestry of habits, and no habit is more important to your spiritual health than the discipline of daily prayer and devotion to the Creator. When you begin each day with your head bowed and your heart lifted, you are reminded of God's love and God's laws.

When you do engage in a regular regime of worship and praise, God will reward you for your wisdom and your obedience. Each new day is a gift from God, and if you're wise, you'll spend a few quiet moments thanking the Giver. It's a wonderful way to start your day.

A person with no devotional life generally struggles with faith and obedience.

Charles Stanley

Mark it down. God never turns away the honest seeker. Go to God with your questions. You may not find all the answers, but in finding God, you know the One who does.

Max Lucado

Maintenance of the devotional mood is indispensable to success in the Christian life.

A. W. Tozer

TODAY'S PRAYER

Dear Lord, I know that it's important to talk to You every day. So even when I'm busy, I will slow myself down long enough to study Your Word and ask for Your guidance. Amen

THE CHOICE TO DATE PEOPLE WHO KNOW GOD

We must obey God rather than men.
Acts 5:29 HCSB

Is God a part of your dating life? Hopefully so. If you sincerely want to know God, then you should date people who feel the same way.

If you're still searching for Mr. or Mrs. Right (while trying to avoid falling in love with Mr. or Mrs. Wrong), be patient, be prudent, and be picky. Look for someone whose values you respect, whose behavior you approve of, and whose faith you admire. Remember that appearances can be deceiving and tempting, so watch your step. And when it comes to the important task of building a lifetime relationship with the guy or girl of your dreams, pray about it!

When it comes to your dating life, God wants to give His approval—or not—but He won't give it until He's asked. So ask, listen, and decide accordingly.

We discover our role in life through our relationships with others.

Rick Warren

Make God's will the focus of your life day by day. If you seek to please Him and Him alone, you'll find yourself satisfied with life.

Kay Arthur

It wasn't the apple, it was the pair.

Anonymous

Line by line, moment by moment, special times are etched into our memories in the permanent ink of everlasting love in our relationships.

Gloria Gaither

TODAY'S PRAYER

Lord, I will let You rule over every aspect of my life, including my relationships. And I know that when I do, You will help me make choices that are right for me, today and every day that I live. Amen

PRAISE HIM!

I will praise You with my whole heart.
Psalm 138:1 NKJV

If you're like most folks on the planet, you're busy. Your life is probably hectic, demanding, and complicated. And when the demands of life leave you rushing from place to place with scarcely a moment to spare, you may not take time to praise your Creator. Big mistake.

The Bible makes it clear: it pays to praise God. Worship and praise should be a part of everything you do. Otherwise, you quickly lose perspective as you fall prey to the demands of everyday life.

Do you sincerely desire to know God in a more meaningful way? Then praise Him for who He is and for what He has done for you. And please don't wait until Sunday morning—praise Him all day long, every day, for as long as you live . . . and then for all eternity.

Two wings are necessary to lift our souls toward God: prayer and praise. Prayer asks. Praise accepts the answer.

Mrs. Charles E. Cowman

Praise opens the window of our hearts, preparing us to walk more closely with God. Prayer raises the window of our spirit, enabling us to listen more clearly to the Father.

Max Lucado

Most of the verses written about praise in God's Word were voiced by people faced with crushing heartaches, injustice, treachery, slander, and scores of other difficult situations.

Joni Eareckson Tada

TODAY'S PRAYER

Heavenly Father, today and every day I will praise You. I will praise You with my thoughts, my prayers, my words, and my deeds . . . now and forever. Amen

DURING DIFFICULT DAYS

*God is our refuge and strength,
a helper who is always found in times of trouble.*
Psalm 46:1 HCSB

All of us face difficult days. Sometimes even the most devout Christians can become discouraged, and you are no exception. After all, you live in a world where expectations can be high and demands can be even higher.

If you find yourself enduring difficult circumstances, remember that God remains in His heaven. If you become discouraged with the direction of your day or your life, turn your thoughts and prayers to Him. He is a God of possibility, not negativity. He will guide you through your difficulties and beyond them. And then, with a renewed spirit of optimism and hope, you can thank the Giver of all things good for gifts that are simply too numerous to count.

When life is difficult, God wants us to have a faith that trusts and waits.

Kay Arthur

The strengthening of faith comes from staying with it in the hour of trial. We should not shrink from tests of faith.

Catherine Marshall

Our heavenly Father never takes anything from his children unless he means to give them something better.

George Mueller

TODAY'S PRAYER

Lord, on difficult days, I will turn to You for my strength. In times of sadness, I will put my trust in You. In times of frustration, I will find peace in You. And every day, whether I am happy or sad, I will praise You for Your glorious works and for the gift of Your Son. Amen

A WORTHY DISCIPLE

*He has told you men what is good and what it is
the Lord requires of you: Only to act justly, to love
faithfulness, and to walk humbly with your God.*

Micah 6:8 HCSB

When Jesus addressed His disciples, He warned
that each one must, "take up his cross and follow me." The disciples must have known exactly
what the Master meant. In Jesus' day, prisoners
were forced to carry their own crosses to the lo-
cation where they would be put to death. Thus,
Christ's message was clear: in order to follow
Him, Christ's disciples must deny themselves
and, instead, trust Him completely. Nothing has
changed since then.

If we are to be disciples of Christ, we must
trust Him and place Him at very the center of
our beings. Jesus never comes "next." He is always first.

Discipleship is a daily discipline: we follow Jesus a step at a time, a day at a time.

Warren Wiersbe

Discipleship is a decision to live by what I know about God, not by what I feel about him or myself or my neighbors.

Eugene Peterson

Discipleship means allegiance to the suffering Christ, and it is therefore not at all surprising that Christians should be called upon to suffer.

Dietrich Bonhoeffer

TODAY'S PRAYER

Help me, Lord, to understand what cross I am to bear this day. Give me the strength and the courage to carry that cross along the path of Your choosing so that I may be a worthy disciple of Your Son. Amen

73

CONTROLLING YOUR TEMPER

My dear brothers and sisters, be quick to listen,
slow to speak, and slow to get angry. Your anger
can never make things right in God's sight.

James 1:19-20 NLT

Temper tantrums are usually unproductive, unattractive, unforgettable, and unnecessary. Perhaps that's why Proverbs 16:32 states that, "Controlling your temper is better than capturing a city" (NCV).

If you've allowed anger to become a regular visitor at your house, you should pray for wisdom, for patience, and for a heart that is so filled with forgiveness that it contains no room for bitterness. God will help you terminate your tantrums if you ask Him to—and that's a good thing because anger and peace cannot coexist in the same mind.

If you permit yourself to become angry, you will forfeit—at least for now—the peace that might otherwise be yours through Christ. So obey God's Word by turning away from anger today and every day. You'll be glad you did, and so will your family and friends.

Life is too short to spend it being angry, bored, or dull.

Barbara Johnson

Anger unresolved will only bring you woe.

Kay Arthur

When you strike out in anger, you may miss the other person, but you will always hit yourself.

Jim Gallery

TODAY'S PRAYER

Dear Lord, when I become angry, help me to remember that You offer me peace and patience. I'll look to You, God, for wisdom, for patience, and for the peace that only You can give. Amen

THE SIMPLE LIFE

*Whoever becomes simple and elemental again,
like this child, will rank high in God's kingdom.*

Matthew 18:4 MSG

Want to reduce stress? Here's a simple solution: Simplify your life. Unfortunately, it's easier said than done. After all, you live in a world where simplicity is in short supply.

Think for a moment about the complexity of your everyday life and compare it to the lives of your ancestors. Certainly, you are the beneficiary of many technological innovations, but those innovations have a price: in all likelihood, your world is highly complex. Unless you take firm control of your time and your life, you may be overwhelmed by a stress-inducing tidal wave of complexity that threatens your happiness.

Your Heavenly Father understands the joy of living simply, and so should you. So do yourself a favor: Keep your life as simple as possible. Simplicity is, indeed, genius. By simplifying your life, you are destined to improve it.

It is the simple things of life that make living worthwhile, the sweet fundamental things such as love and duty, work and rest, and living close to nature.

Laura Ingalls Wilder

It is part of Satan's program to make our faith complicated and involved. Now and then, we need a rediscovery of the simplicity that is in Christ and in our faith in Him.

Vance Havner

Simplicity reaches out after God; purity discovers and enjoys him.

Thomas à Kempis

TODAY'S PRAYER

Dear Lord, life is complicated enough without my adding to the confusion. Help me understand the wisdom of simplicity. Wherever I happen to be, help me to keep it simple—very simple. Amen

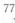

AIM HIGH

*I can do everything through him
that gives me strength.*

Philippians 4:13 NIV

It takes courage to dream big dreams. You will discover that courage when you do three things: accept the past, trust God to handle the future, and make the most of the time He has given you today.

Are you excited about the opportunities of today and thrilled by the possibilities of tomorrow? Do you confidently expect God to lead you to a place of abundance, peace, and joy? And, when your days on earth are over, do you expect to receive the priceless gift of eternal life? If you trust God's promises, and if you have welcomed God's Son into your heart, then you should believe that your future is intensely and eternally bright.

No dreams are too big for God—not even yours. So start living—and dreaming—accordingly.

You cannot out-dream God.

John Eldredge

Always stay connected to people and seek out things that bring you joy. Dream with abandon. Pray confidently.

Barbara Johnson

The future lies all before us. Shall it only be a slight advance upon what we usually do? Ought it not to be a bound, a leap forward to altitudes of endeavor and success undreamed of before?

Annie Armstrong

TODAY'S PRAYER

Dear Lord, give me the courage to dream and the faithfulness to trust in Your perfect plan for my life. When I am worried, give me strength for today and hope for tomorrow. Today, Father, I will trust You and honor You with my thoughts, with my prayers, with my actions, and with my dreams. Amen

THE WISDOM
TO BE GENEROUS

Freely you have received, freely give.
Matthew 10:8 NIV

God's gifts are beyond description, His blessings beyond comprehension. God has been incredibly generous with us, and He rightfully expects us to be generous with others. That's why the thread of generosity is woven into the very fabric of God's teachings.

In the Old Testament, we are told that, "The good person is generous and lends lavishly...." (Psalm 112:5 MSG). And in the New Testament we are instructed, "Freely you have received, freely give" (Matthew 10:8 NKJV). These principles still apply. As we establish priorities for our days and our lives, we are advised to give freely of our time, our possessions, and our love—just as God has given freely to us.

Of course, we can never fully repay God for His gifts, but we can share them with others. And we should.

The measure of a life, after all, is not its duration but its donation.

Corrie ten Boom

Nothing is really ours until we share it.

C. S. Lewis

A happy spirit takes the grind out of giving. The grease of gusto frees the gears of generosity.

Charles Swindoll

The mind grows by taking in, but the heart grows by giving out.

Warren Wiersbe

TODAY'S PRAYER

Lord, make me a generous and cheerful Christian. Let me be kind to those who need my encouragement, and let me share with those who need my help, today and every day. Amen

THE IMPORTANCE OF ENCOURAGEMENT

Pleasant words are like a honeycomb,
Sweetness to the soul and health to the bones.
Proverbs 16:24 NKJV

Life is a team sport, and all of us need occasional pats on the back from our teammates. As Christians, we are called upon to spread the Good News of Christ, and we are also called to spread a message of encouragement and hope to the world.

Whether you realize it or not, many people with whom you come in contact every day are in desperate need of a smile or an encouraging word. The world can be a difficult place, and countless friends and family members may be troubled by the challenges of everyday life. Since you don't always know who needs your help, the best strategy is to try to encourage all the people who cross your path. So today, be a world-class source of encouragement to everyone you meet. Never has the need been greater.

We can never untangle all the woes in other people's lives. We can't produce miracles overnight. But we can bring a cup of cool water to a thirsty soul, or a scoop of laughter to a lonely heart.

Barbara Johnson

How many people stop because so few say, "Go!"

Charles Swindoll

I can usually sense that a leading is from the Holy Spirit when it calls me to humble myself, to serve somebody, to encourage somebody, or to give something away. Very rarely will the evil one lead us to do those kind of things.

Bill Hybels

TODAY'S PRAYER

Dear Lord, help me remember that I should always be an encouraging person. Make me a powerful source of encouragement to people in need, and let my words and actions be worthy of Your Son. Amen

83

CONTAGIOUS FAITH

Whatever you do, do it enthusiastically,
as something done for the Lord and not for men.
Colossians 3:23 HCSB

The stronger your faith, the better you can rise above the inevitable stresses of everyday life. And the more enthused you are about your faith, the better you can share it.

Are you genuinely excited about your faith? And do you make your enthusiasm known to those around you? Or are you a "silent ambassador" for Christ? God's preference is clear: He intends that you stand before others and proclaim your faith.

Genuine, heartfelt Christianity is contagious. If you enjoy a life-altering relationship with God, that relationship will have an impact on others— perhaps a profound impact.

Does Christ reign over your life? Then share your testimony and your excitement. The world needs both.

We act as though comfort and luxury were the chief requirements of life, when all we need to make us really happy is something to be enthusiastic about.

Charles Kingsley

Your enthusiasm will be infectious, stimulating, and attractive to others. They will love you for it. They will go for you and with you.

Norman Vincent Peale

Don't take hold of a thing unless you want that thing to take hold of you.

E. Stanley Jones

TODAY'S PRAYER

Dear Lord, the Christian life is a glorious adventure—let me share my excitement with others. Let me be an enthusiastic believer, Father, and let me share my enthusiasm today and every day. Amen

BEYOND ENVY

*Therefore, laying aside all malice, all deceit,
hypocrisy, envy, and all evil speaking,
as newborn babes, desire the pure milk of the word,
that you may grow thereby.*
1 Peter 2:1-2 NKJV

Because we are frail, imperfect human beings, we are sometimes envious of others. But God's Word warns us that envy is sin. Thus, we must guard ourselves against the natural tendency to feel resentment and jealousy when other people experience good fortune. As believers, we have absolutely no reason to be envious of any people on earth. After all, as Christians we are already recipients of the greatest gift in all creation: God's grace. We have been promised the gift of eternal life through God's only begotten Son, and we must count that gift as our most precious possession.

So here's a simple suggestion that is guaranteed to bring you happiness: fill your heart with

God's love, God's promises, and God's Son . . . and when you do so, leave no room for envy, hatred, bitterness, or regret.

How can you possess the miseries of envy when you possess in Christ the best of all portions?

C. H. Spurgeon

What God asks, does, or requires of others is not my business; it is His.

Kay Arthur

Discontent dries up the soul.

Elisabeth Elliot

TODAY'S PRAYER

Dear Lord, You are the Giver of all good gifts. Today I will praise You for my blessings, and I won't be envious of the blessings You've given to others. Amen

BE A GOOD EXAMPLE

For am I now trying to win the favor of people,
or God? Or am I striving to please people?
If I were still trying to please people,
I would not be a slave of Christ.
Galatians 1:10 HCSB

Whether you like it or not, you simply can't deny the fact that you're an example to other people. The question is not whether you will be an example to your family and friends; the question is precisely what kind of example will you be.

Corrie ten Boom advised, "Don't worry about what you do not understand. Worry about what you do understand in the Bible but do not live by." And that's sound advice because your family, friends, and dates are always watching . . . and so, for that matter, is God.

Too many Christians have geared their program to please, to entertain, and to gain favor from this world. We are concerned with how much, instead of how little, like this age we can become.

Billy Graham

Nothing speaks louder or more powerfully than a life of integrity.

Charles Swindoll

In your desire to share the gospel, you may be the only Jesus someone else will ever meet. Be real and be involved with people.

Barbara Johnson

TODAY'S PRAYER

Lord, make me a worthy example to my family and friends. And, let my words and my actions show people how my life has been changed by You. I will praise You, Father, by following in the footsteps of Your Son. Let others see Him through me. Amen

EXPECT HIS ABUNDANCE

I have come that they may have life,
and that they may have it more abundantly.
John 10:10 NKJV

When Jesus talks of the abundant life, is He talking about material riches or earthly fame? Hardly. The Son of God came to this world, not to give it prosperity, but to give it salvation. Thankfully for Christians, our Savior's abundance is both spiritual and eternal; it never falters—even if we do—and it never dies.

God's gifts are available to all, but they are not guaranteed; those gifts must be claimed by those who choose to follow Christ. As believers, we are free to accept God's gifts, or not; that choice, and the consequences that result from it, are ours and ours alone.

As we go about our daily lives, may we accept God's promise of spiritual abundance, and may we share it with a world in desperate need of the Master's healing touch.

If we just give God the little that we have, we can trust Him to make it go around.

Gloria Gaither

If we were given all we wanted here, our hearts would settle for this world rather than the next.

Elisabeth Elliot

God is the giver, and we are the receivers. And His richest gifts are bestowed not upon those who do the greatest things, but upon those who accept His abundance and His grace.

Hannah Whitall Smith

TODAY'S PRAYER

Dear Lord, You have offered me the gift of abundance through Your Son. Thank You, Father, for the abundant life that is mine through Christ Jesus. Let me accept His gifts and use them always to glorify You. Amen

BITTERNESS PUTS DISTANCE BETWEEN YOU AND GOD

*All bitterness, anger and wrath, insult and slander
must be removed from you, along with
all wickedness. And be kind and compassionate
to one another, forgiving one another,
just as God also forgave you in Christ.*
Ephesians 4:31-32 HCSB

If you're unwilling to forgive other people, you're building a roadblock between yourself and God. And the less you're willing to forgive, the bigger your roadblock. So if you want to know God in a more meaningful way, you must learn how to forgive and, to the best of your abilities, forget.

Is there someone out there you need to forgive? If so, pray for that person. And then pray for yourself by asking God to heal your heart. Don't expect forgiveness to be easy or quick, but rest assured: with God as your partner, you can forgive . . . and you will.

By not forgiving, by not letting wrongs go, we aren't getting back at anyone. We are merely punishing ourselves by barricading our own hearts.

Jim Cymbala

Bitterness is a spiritual cancer, a rapidly growing malignancy that can consume your life. Bitterness cannot be ignored but must be healed at the very core, and only Christ can heal bitterness.

Beth Moore

TODAY'S PRAYER

Heavenly Father, free me from anger and bitterness. When I am angry, I cannot feel the peace that You intend for my life. When I am bitter, I cannot sense Your presence. Let me turn away from bitterness and instead claim the spiritual abundance that You offer through the gift of Your Son. Amen

CHOOSING TO BE A CHEERFUL CHRISTIAN

A cheerful heart has a continual feast.
Proverbs 15:15 HCSB

Few things in life are more sad, or, for that matter, more absurd, than a grumpy Christian. Christ promises us lives of abundance and joy, but He does not force His joy upon us. We must claim His joy for ourselves, and when we do, Jesus, in turn, fills our spirits with His power and His love.

How can we receive from Christ the joy that is rightfully ours? By giving Him what is rightfully His: our hearts and our souls.

When we earnestly commit ourselves to the Savior of mankind, when we place Jesus at the center of our lives and trust Him as our personal Savior, He will transform us, not just for today, but for all eternity. Then we, as God's children, can share Christ's joy and His message with a world that needs both.

Be assured, my dear friend, that it is no joy to God in seeing you with a dreary countenance.

C. H. Spurgeon

The people whom I have seen succeed best in life have always been cheerful and hopeful people who went about their business with a smile on their faces.

Charles Kingsley

Christ can put a spring in your step and a thrill in your heart. Optimism and cheerfulness are products of knowing Christ.

Billy Graham

TODAY'S PRAYER

Dear Lord, I have so many blessings. Help me count those blessings and be glad. And, let Your love live in my heart this day and forever. Amen

THE LESSONS OF TOUGH TIMES

If you hide your sins, you will not succeed.
If you confess and reject them,
you will receive mercy.

Proverbs 28:13 NCV

Everybody makes mistakes, and so will you. In fact, Winston Churchill once observed, "Success is going from failure to failure without loss of enthusiasm." What was good for Churchill is also good for you. You should expect to make mistakes—plenty of mistakes—but you should not allow those missteps to rob you of the enthusiasm you need to fulfill God's plan for your life.

We are imperfect people living in an imperfect world; mistakes are simply part of the price we pay for being here. But, even though mistakes are an inevitable part of life's journey, repeated mistakes should not be. When we commit the inevitable blunders of life, we must correct them, learn from them, and pray for the wisdom not to repeat them. When we do, our mistakes become lessons, and our lives become adventures in growth, not stagnation.

Have you made a mistake or three? Of course you have. But here's the big question: have you used your mistakes as stumbling blocks or stepping stones? The answer to that question will determine how well you will perform in every aspect of your life.

Very few things motivate us to give God our undivided attention like being faced with the negative consequences of our decisions.

Charles Stanley

TODAY'S PRAYER

Dear Lord, there's a right way to do things and a wrong way to do things. When I do things that are wrong, help me be quick to ask for forgiveness . . . and quick to correct my mistakes. Amen

DEFEATING NEGATIVITY

*Let angry people endure the backlash
of their own anger; if you try to make it better,
you'll only make it worse.*

Proverbs 19:19 MSG

From experience, we know that it is easy to criticize others. And we know that it is usually far easier to find faults than to find solutions. Still, the urge to criticize others remains a powerful temptation for most of us.

Negativity is highly contagious: We give it to others who, in turn, give it back to us. This stress-inducing cycle can be broken only by positive thoughts, heartfelt prayers, encouraging words, and meaningful acts of kindness.

As thoughtful servants of a loving God, we have no valid reason—and no legitimate excuse—to be negative. So, when we are tempted to be overly critical of others, or unfairly critical of ourselves, we must use the transforming power of God's love to break the chains of negativity. We must defeat negativity before negativity defeats us.

Winners see an answer for every problem; losers see a problem in every answer.

Barbara Johnson

To lose heart is to lose everything.

John Eldredge

After one hour in heaven, we shall be ashamed that we ever grumbled.

Vance Havner

TODAY'S PRAYER

Lord, give me faith, optimism, and hope. Let me expect the best from You, and let me look for the best in others. Let me trust You, Lord, to direct my life. And, let me be Your faithful, hopeful, optimistic servant every day that I live. Amen

GIMME PATIENCE!

Be gentle to everyone, able to teach, and patient.
2 Timothy 2:23 HCSB

Are you a perfectly patient person? If so, feel free to skip the rest of this page. But if you're not, here's something to think about: If you really want to become a more patient person, God is ready and willing to help.

The Bible promises that when you sincerely seek God's help, He will give you the things that you need—and that includes patience. But God won't force you to become a more patient person. If you want to become a more mature Christian, you've got to do some of the work yourself—and the best time to start doing that work is now.

So, if you want to gain patience and maturity, bow your head and start praying about it. Then, rest assured that with God's help, you can most certainly make yourself a more patient, understanding, mature Christian.

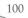

As we wait on God, He helps us use the winds of adversity to soar above our problems. As the Bible says, "Those who wait on the LORD…shall mount up with wings like eagles."

Billy Graham

You can't step in front of God and not get in trouble. When He says, "Go three steps," don't go four.

Charles Stanley

Be patient. God is using today's difficulties to strengthen you for tomorrow. He is equipping you. The God who makes things grow will help you bear fruit.

Max Lucado

TODAY'S PRAYER

Lord, sometimes I can be a very impatient person. Slow me down and calm me down. Let me trust in Your plan, Father; let me trust in Your timetable; and let me trust in Your love for me. Amen

FINDING PEACE

These things I have spoken to you,
that in Me you may have peace. In the world you
will have tribulation; but be of good cheer,
I have overcome the world.

John 16:33 NKJV

Oftentimes, our outer struggles are simply manifestations of the inner conflict that we feel when we stray from God's path. Jesus offers us peace, not as the world gives, but as He alone gives. Our challenge is to accept Christ's peace into our hearts and then, as best we can, to share His peace with our neighbors. When we accept Jesus as our personal Savior, we are transformed by His grace. We are then free to accept the spiritual abundance and peace that can be ours through the power of the risen Christ.

Have you found the genuine peace that can be yours through Jesus Christ? Or are you still rushing after the illusion of "peace and happiness" that the world promises but cannot deliver?

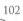

Today, as a gift to yourself, to your family, and to your friends, claim the inner peace that is your spiritual birthright: the peace of Jesus Christ. It is offered freely; it has been paid for in full; it is yours for the asking. So ask. And then share.

Prayer guards hearts and minds and causes God to bring peace out of chaos.

Beth Moore

The fruit of our placing all things in God's hands is the presence of His abiding peace in our hearts.

Hannah Whitall Smith

TODAY'S PRAYER

Dear Lord, I will open my heart to You. And I thank You, God, for Your love, for Your peace, and for Your Son. Amen

AVOID THE WRONG KIND OF PEER PRESSURE

Whoever walks with the wise will become wise;
whoever walks with fools will suffer harm.

Proverbs 13:20 NLT

Who you are depends, to a surprising extent, on the people you hang out with. Peer pressure can be good or bad, depending upon who your peers are and how they behave. If your friends encourage you to follow God's will and to obey His commandments, then you'll experience positive peer pressure, and that's a good thing. But, if your friends encourage you to do foolish things, then you're facing a different kind of peer pressure . . . and you'd better beware.

Do you want to feel good about yourself and your life? If so, here's a simple, proven strategy: go out and find friends who, by their words and their actions, will help you build the kind of life that's worth feeling good about.

Nothing can be more dangerous than keeping wicked companions. They communicate the infection of their vices to all who associate with them.

St. Jean Baptiste de la Salle

Choose the opposition of the whole world rather than offend Jesus.

Thomas à Kempis

You'll probably end up behaving like your friends behave . . . and if that's a scary thought, it time to make a new set of friends.

Criswell Freeman

TODAY'S PRAYER

Dear Lord, other people may encourage me to stray from Your path, but I wish to follow in the footsteps of Your Son. Give me the vision to see the right path—and the wisdom to follow it—today and every day of my life. Amen

105

DAY 50

GOOD DECISION

If you need wisdom— if you want to know what God wants you to do—ask him, and he will gladly tell you. He will not resent your asking.

James 1:5 NLT

Everyday life is an adventure in decision-making. Each day, we make countless decisions that hopefully bring us closer to God. When we obey God's commandments, we share in His abundance and His peace. But, when we turn our backs upon God by disobeying Him, we invite Old Man Trouble to stop by for an extended visit.

Do you want to be successful and happy? If so, here's a good place to start: Obey God. When you're faced with a difficult choice or a powerful temptation, pray about it. Invite God into your heart and live according to His commandments. When you do, you will be blessed today, and tomorrow, and forever.

If we don't hunger and thirst after righteousness, we'll become anemic and feel miserable in our Christian experience.

Franklin Graham

Righteousness not only defines God, but God defines righteousness.

Bill Hybels

The Reference Point for the Christian is the Bible. All values, judgments, and attitudes must be gauged in relationship to this Reference Point.

Ruth Bell Graham

TODAY'S PRAYER

Lord, help me to make decisions that are pleasing to You. Help me to be honest, patient, thoughtful, and obedient. And above all, help me to follow the teachings of Jesus, not just today, but every day. Amen

HE ANSWERS

*If you believe, you will receive whatever
you ask for in prayer.*
Matthew 21:22 NIV

In case you've been wondering, wonder no more—God does answer your prayers. What God does not do is this: He does not always answer your prayers as soon as you might like, and He does not always answer your prayers by saying "Yes."

God isn't an order-taker, and He's not some sort of cosmic vending machine. Sometimes—even when we want something very badly—our loving Heavenly Father responds to our requests by saying "No," and we must accept His answer, even if we don't understand it.

God answers prayers not only according to our wishes but also according to His master plan. We cannot know that plan, but we can know the Planner . . . and we must trust His wisdom, His righteousness, and His love.

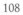

Avail yourself of the greatest privilege this side of heaven: prayer. Jesus Christ died to make this communion and communication with the Father possible.

Billy Graham

When you ask God to do something, don't ask timidly; put your whole heart into it.

Marie T. Freeman

Are you weak? Weary? Confused? Troubled? Pressured? How is your relationship with God? Is it held in its place of priority? I believe the greater the pressure, the greater your need for time alone with Him.

Kay Arthur

TODAY'S PRAYER

Lord, make me a prayerful Christian. In good times and in bad times, in whatever state I find myself, let me turn my prayers to You. You always hear my prayers, God; let me always pray them! Amen

HE IS SUFFICIENT

The Lord is my rock, my fortress, and my deliverer
Psalm 18:2 HCSB

It is easy to become overwhelmed by the demands of life, but if you're a faithful follower of Christ, you need never be overwhelmed. Why? Because God's love is sufficient to meet your needs. Whatever dangers you may face, whatever heartbreaks you must endure, God is with you, and He stands ready to comfort you and to heal you.

The Psalmist writes, "Weeping may endure for a night, but joy comes in the morning" (Psalm 30:5 NKJV). But when we are suffering, the morning may seem very far away. It is not. God promises that He is "near to those who have a broken heart" (Psalm 34:18 NKJV).

If you are experiencing the intense pain of a recent loss, or if you are still mourning a loss from long ago, perhaps you are now ready to begin the next stage of your journey with God. If so, be mindful of this fact: the loving heart of God is sufficient to meet any challenge, including yours.

God is always sufficient in perfect proportion to our need.

Beth Moore

God will call you to obey Him and do whatever he asks of you. However, you do not need to be doing something to feel fulfilled. You are fulfilled completely in a relationship with God. When you are filled with Him, what else do you need?

Henry Blackaby and Claude King

Faith is not merely you holding on to God—it is God holding on to you.

E. Stanley Jones

TODAY'S PRAYER

Dear Lord, You are sufficient for my needs, and I praise You. I will turn to You when I am fearful or worried. You are my loving Heavenly Father, sufficient in all things and I will trust You always. Amen

A GOOD ATTITUDE PAYS BIG DIVIDENDS

*Finally brothers, whatever is true, whatever is
honorable, whatever is just, whatever is pure,
whatever is lovely, whatever is commendable—
if there is any moral excellence and
if there is any praise—dwell on these things.*

Philippians 4:8 HCSB

How will you direct your thoughts today? Will
you obey the words of Philippians 4:8 by dwelling
upon those things that are honorable, just, and
commendable? Or will you allow your thoughts
to be hijacked by the negativity that seems to
dominate our troubled world? Are you fearful,
angry, stressed, or worried? Are you so preoccupied with the concerns of this day that you fail to
thank God for the promise of eternity? Are you
confused, bitter, or pessimistic? If so, God wants
to have a little talk with you.

God intends that you experience joy and
abundance. So, today and every day hereafter,

celebrate the life that God has given you by focusing your thoughts upon those things that are worthy of praise. Today, count your blessings instead of your hardships. And thank the Giver of all things good for gifts that are simply too numerous to count.

The things we think are the things that feed our souls. If we think on pure and lovely things, we shall grow pure and lovely like them; and the converse is equally true.

Hannah Whitall Smith

TODAY'S PRAYER

Lord, I pray for an attitude that is Christlike. Whatever my circumstances, whether good or bad, triumphal or tragic, let my response reflect a God-honoring attitude of optimism, faith, and love for You. Amen

HE RENEWS OUR STRENGTH

*He gives strength to the weary and
strengthens the powerless.*
Isaiah 40:29 HCSB

When we genuinely lift our hearts and prayers to God, He renews our strength. Are you almost too stressed to lift your head? Then bow it. Offer your concerns and your fears to your Father in Heaven. He is always at your side, offering His love and His strength.

Are you troubled or anxious? Take your anxieties to God in prayer. Are you weak or worried? Delve deeply into God's Holy Word and sense His presence in the quiet moments of the day. Are you spiritually exhausted? Call upon fellow believers to support you, and call upon Christ to renew your spirit and your life. Your Savior will never let you down. To the contrary, He will always lift you up if you ask Him to. So what, dear friend, are you waiting for?

He is the God of wholeness and restoration.

Stormie Omartian

Repentance removes old sins and wrong attitudes, and it opens the way for the Holy Spirit to restore our spiritual health.

Shirley Dobson

When we reach the end of our strength, wisdom, and personal resources, we enter into the beginning of his glorious provisions.

Patsy Clairmont

TODAY'S PRAYER

Dear Lord, You can make all things new. I am a new creature in Christ Jesus, and when I fall short in my commitment, You can renew my effort and my enthusiasm. When I am weak or worried, restore my strength, Lord, for my own sake and for the sake of Your kingdom. Amen

115

ENTRUSTING THE FUTURE TO GOD

"I say this because I know what I am planning for you," says the Lord. "I have good plans for you, not plans to hurt you. I will give you hope and a good future."

Jeremiah 29:11 NCV

How can you make smart choices if you're unwilling to trust God and obey Him? The answer, of course, is that you can't. That's why you should trust God in everything (and that means entrusting your future to God).

How bright is your future? Well, if you're a faithful believer, God's plans for you are so bright that you'd better wear shades. But here are some important follow-up questions: How bright do you believe your future to be? Are you expecting a terrific tomorrow, or are you dreading a terrible one? The answer you give will have a powerful impact on the way tomorrow turns out.

Do you trust in the ultimate goodness of God's plan for your life? Will you face tomorrow's challenges with optimism and hope? You should. After all, God created you for a very important reason: His reason. And you have important work to do: His work.

Today, as you live in the present and look to the future, remember that God has an amazing plan for you. Act—and believe—accordingly.

We must trust as if it all depended on God and work as if it all depended on us.

C. H.. Spurgeon

The Christian believes in a fabulous future.

Billy Graham

TODAY'S PRAYER

Dear Lord, sometimes when I think about the future, I worry. Today, I will do a better job of trusting You. You are my Father, and I will place my hope and my faith in You. Amen

THINK AHEAD

I will instruct you and teach you in the way you
should go; I will guide you with My eye.
Psalm 32:8 NKJV

Maybe you've heard this old saying: "Look before you leap." Well, that saying may be old, but it still applies to you. Before you jump into something, you should look ahead and plan ahead. Otherwise, you might soon be sorry you jumped!

When you acquire the habit of thinking ahead and planning ahead, you'll make better choices (and, as a result, you'll feel better about yourself).

So when it comes to the important things in life, don't allow impulsive behavior to dynamite your future. Think long and hard about the consequences of your actions before you do something foolish . . . or dangerous . . . or both.

It's incredible to realize that what we do each day has meaning in the big picture of God's plan.

Bill Hybels

Allow your dreams a place in your prayers and plans. God-given dreams can help you move into the future He is preparing for you.

Barbara Johnson

The only way you can experience abundant life is to surrender your plans to Him.

Charles Stanley

Sometimes, being wise is nothing more than slowing down long enough to think about things before you do them.

Marie T. Freeman

TODAY'S PRAYER

Lord, sometimes I can be an impulsive person. Slow me down, calm me down, and help me make wise decisions . . . today and every day of my life. Amen

USING YOUR GIFTS

*I remind you to keep ablaze the gift of God
that is in you.*
2 Timothy 1:6 HCSB

How do we thank God for the gifts He has given us? By using those gifts, that's how!

God has given you talents and opportunities that are uniquely yours. Are you willing to use your gifts in the way that God intends? And are you willing to summon the discipline that is required to develop your talents and to hone your skills? That's precisely what God wants you to do, and that's precisely what you should desire for yourself.

As you seek to expand your talents, you will undoubtedly encounter stumbling blocks along the way, such as the fear of rejection or the fear of failure. When you do, don't stumble! Just continue to refine your skills, and offer your services to God. And when the time is right, He will use you—but it's up to you to be thoroughly prepared when He does.

You are the only person on earth who can use your ability.

Zig Ziglar

God often reveals His direction for our lives through the way He made us . . . with a certain personality and unique skills.

Bill Hybels

The Lord has abundantly blessed me all of my life. I'm not trying to pay Him back for all of His wonderful gifts; I just realize that He gave them to me to give away.

Lisa Whelchel

TODAY'S PRAYER

Lord, I praise You for Your priceless gifts. I give thanks for Your creation, for Your Son, and for the unique talents and opportunities that You have given me. Let me use my gifts for the glory of Your kingdom, this day and every day. Amen

121

THE CHOICE TO PUT GOD FIRST

You shall have no other gods before Me.

Exodus 20:3 NKJV

Who is in charge of your heart? Is it God, or is it something else? Have you given Christ your heart, your soul, your talents, your time, and your testimony? Or are you giving Him little more than a few hours each Sunday morning?

In the book of Exodus, God warns that we should place no gods before Him. Yet all too often, we place our Lord in second, third, or fourth place as we worship other things. When we unwittingly place possessions or relationships above our love for the Creator, we create big problems for ourselves.

Have you chosen to allow God to rule your heart? Make certain that the honest answer to this question is a resounding yes. In the life of every thoughtful believer, God comes first. That's precisely the place that He deserves in your heart.

One with God is a majority.

Billy Graham

God is the beyond in the midst of our life.

Dietrich Bonhoeffer

You can't get second things by putting them first; you can get second things only by putting first things first.

C. S. Lewis

We become whatever we are committed to.

Rick Warren

TODAY'S PRAYER

Dear Lord, keep me mindful of the need to place You first in every aspect of my life. You have blessed me beyond measure, Father, and I will praise You with my thoughts, my prayers, my testimony, and my service, this day and every day. Amen

GOD IS LOVE

God is love, and the one who remains
in love remains in God,
and God remains in him.
1 John 4:16 HCSB

The Bible makes this promise: God is love. It's a sweeping statement, a profoundly important description of what God is and how God works. God's love is perfect. When we open our hearts to His perfect love, we are touched by the Creator's hand, and we are transformed.

Today, even if you can only carve out a few quiet moments, offer sincere prayers of thanksgiving to your Creator. He loves you now and throughout all eternity. Open your heart to His presence and His love.

The life of faith is a daily exploration of the constant and countless ways in which God's grace and love are experienced.

Eugene Peterson

If you have an obedience problem, you have a love problem. Focus your attention on God's love.

Henry Blackaby

I can tell you, from personal experience of walking with God for over fifty years, that He is the Lover of my soul.

Vonette Bright

TODAY'S PRAYER

Dear Lord, the Bible teaches me that You are love. And, I know that You love me. I will accept Your love—and share it—today and every day. Amen

LET GOD GUIDE THE WAY

The true children of God are those who let God's Spirit lead them.

Romans 8:14 NCV

The Bible promises that God will guide you if you let Him. Your job is to let Him. But sometimes, you will be tempted to do otherwise. Sometimes, you'll be tempted to go along with the crowd; other times, you'll be tempted to do things your way, not God's way. When you feel these temptations, resist them.

God has promised that when you ask for His help, He will not withhold it. So ask. Ask Him to meet the needs of your day. Ask Him to lead you, to protect you, and to correct you. And trust the answers He gives.

God stands at the door and waits. When you knock, He opens. When you ask, He answers. Your task, of course, is to seek His guidance prayerfully, confidently, and often.

We have ample evidence that the Lord is able to guide. The promises cover every imaginable situation. All we need to do is to take the hand he stretches out.

Elisabeth Elliot

Only He can guide you to invest your life in worthwhile ways. This guidance will come as you "walk" with Him and listen to Him.

Henry Blackaby and Claude King

Are you serious about wanting God's guidance to become a personal reality in your life? The first step is to tell God that you know you can't manage your own life; that you need his help.

Catherine Marshall

TODAY'S PRAYER

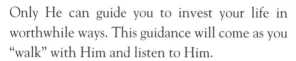

Dear Lord, today I come to You seeking guidance. I will trust You to show me the path that I should take, and I will try, as best I can, to follow in the footsteps of Your Son. Amen

KEEP TRYING TO FIGURE OUT WHAT GOD HAS PLANNED FOR YOU

You will show me the path of life.

Psalm 16:11 NKJV

You'll feel better about yourself if you're living on purpose, not by accident. But sometimes that's hard to do. Why? Because God's plans aren't always clear.

Sometimes we wander aimlessly in a wilderness of our own making. And sometimes, we struggle mightily against God in an unsuccessful attempt to find success and happiness through our own means, not His.

Are you genuinely trying to figure out God's purpose for your life? If so, you can be sure that with God's help, you will eventually discover it. So keep praying, and keep watching. And rest assured: God's got big plans for you . . . very big plans.

God is preparing you as his chosen arrow. As yet your shaft is hidden in his quiver, in the shadows, but, at the precise moment, he will reach for you and launch you to that place of his appointment.

Charles Swindoll

If not a sparrow falls upon the ground without your Father, you have reason to see that the smallest events of your career and your life are arranged by him.

C. H. Spurgeon

With God, it's never "Plan B" or "second best." It's always "Plan A." And, if we let Him, He'll make something beautiful of our lives.

Gloria Gaither

TODAY'S PRAYER

Lord, today, I will seek Your will for my life. You have a plan for me, Father. Let me discover it and live it, knowing that when I trust in You, I am eternally blessed. Amen

INFINITE POSSIBILITIES

Is anything too hard for the LORD?

Genesis 18:14 KJV

Is your faith a little threadbare and worn? If so, it's time to abandon your doubts and reclaim your faith in God's promises.

Ours is a God of infinite possibilities. But sometimes, because of limited faith and limited understanding, we wrongly assume that God cannot or will not intervene in the affairs of mankind. Such assumptions are simply wrong.

God's Holy Word makes it clear: absolutely nothing is impossible for the Lord. And since the Bible means what it says, you can be comforted in the knowledge that the Creator of the universe can do miraculous things in your own life and in the lives of your loved ones. Your challenge, as a believer, is to take God at His word, and to expect the miraculous.

If we take God's program, we can have God's power—not otherwise.

E. Stanley Jones

You can believe in the Holy Spirit not because you see Him, but because you see what He does in people's lives when they are surrendered to Christ and possess His power.

Billy Graham

No giant will ever be a match for a big God with a little rock.

Beth Moore

TODAY'S PRAYER

Heavenly Father, You are all-knowing and all-powerful. Today, I praise You for Your love, and I marvel at the glory of Your Creation. With You as my protector, Lord, I am secure, today and forever. Amen

THE DECISION TO BE HUMBLE

Therefore humble yourselves under the mighty hand of God, that He may exalt you in due time.

1 Peter 5:6 NKJV

On the road to spiritual growth, pride is a massive roadblock. The more prideful you are, the more difficult it is to know God. When you experience success, it's easy to puff out your chest and proclaim, "I did that!" But it's wrong. Dietrich Bonhoeffer was correct when he observed, "It is very easy to overestimate the importance of our own achievements in comparison with what we owe others." In other words, reality breeds humility. So if you want to know God better, be humble. Otherwise, you'll be building a roadblock between you and your Creator (and that's a very bad thing to do!).

Do you wish to rise? Begin by descending. You plan a tower that will pierce the clouds? Lay first the foundation of humility.

St. Augustine

The great characteristic of the saint is humility.

Oswald Chambers

Nothing sets a person so much out of the devil's reach as humility.

Jonathan Edwards

We are never stronger than the moment we admit we are weak.

Beth Moore

TODAY'S PRAYER

Lord, You are great, and I am human. Keep me humble, and keep me mindful that all my gifts come from You. Amen

133

TRUST GOD'S PROMISES

God—His way is perfect;
the word of the Lord is pure.
He is a shield to all who take refuge in Him.

Psalm 18:30 HCSB

God has made quite a few promises to you, and He intends to keep every single one of them. You will find these promises in a book like no other: the Holy Bible. The Bible is your roadmap for life here on earth and for life eternal—as a believer, you are called upon to trust its promises, to follow its commandments, and to share its Good News.

God has made promises to all of humanity and to you. God's promises never fail and they never grow old. You must trust those promises and share them with your family, with your friends, and with the world . . . starting now . . . and ending never.

The stars may fall, but God's promises will stand and be fulfilled.

J. I. Packer

There are four words I wish we would never forget, and they are, "God keeps his word."

Charles Swindoll

The promises of Scripture are not mere pious hopes or sanctified guesses. They are more than sentimental words to be printed on decorated cards for Sunday School children. They are eternal verities. They are true. There is no perhaps about them.

Peter Marshall

TODAY'S PRAYER

Dear God, the Bible contains many promises. Let me trust Your promises, and let me live according to Your Holy Word, not just for today, but forever. Amen

THE ULTIMATE ARMOR

If God is for us, who can be against us?
Romans 8:31 NIV

God has promised to protect us, and He intends to keep His promise. In a world filled with dangers and temptations, God is the ultimate armor. In a world filled with misleading messages, God's Word is the ultimate truth. In a world filled with more frustrations than we can count, God's Son offers the ultimate peace.

Will you accept God's peace and wear God's armor against the dangers of our world? Hopefully so—because when you do, you can live courageously, knowing that you possess the ultimate protection: God's unfailing love for you.

Under heaven's lock and key, we are protected by the most efficient security system available: the power of God.

Charles Swindoll

The Rock of Ages is the great sheltering encirclement.

Oswald Chambers

The Will of God will never take you where the Grace of God will not protect you.

Anonymous

TODAY'S PRAYER

Lord, You are my Shepherd. You care for me; You comfort me; You watch over me; and You have saved me. I will praise You, Father, for Your glorious works, for Your protection, for Your love, and for Your Son. Amen

WHO RULES?

Can you understand the secrets of God? His limits are higher than the heavens; you cannot reach them! They are deeper than the grave; you cannot understand them! His limits are longer than the earth and wider than the sea.

Job 11:7-9 NCV

God reigns over the entire universe, and He reigns over your little corner of that universe. He is sovereign. Your challenge is to recognize God's sovereignty and live in accordance with His commandments. Sometimes, of course, this is easier said than done.

Your Heavenly Father may not always reveal Himself as quickly (or as clearly) as you would like. But rest assured: God is in control, God is here, and God intends to use you in wonderful, unexpected ways. He desires to lead you along a path of His choosing. Your challenge is to watch, to listen, to learn . . . and to follow.

Our God is the sovereign Creator of the universe! He loves us as His own children and has provided every good thing we have; He is worthy of our praise every moment.

Shirley Dobson

The next time you're disappointed, don't panic. Don't give up. Just be patient and let God remind you he's still in control.

Max Lucado

If God is your Co-pilot . . . swap seats!

Anonymous

TODAY'S PRAYER

Dear Lord, You rule over our world, and I will allow You to rule over my heart. I will obey Your commandments, I will study Your Word, and I will seek Your will for my life, today and every day of my life. Amen

PROBLEM-SOLVING 101

People who do what is right may have many problems, but the Lord will solve them all.

Psalm 34:19 NCV

Life is an adventure in problem-solving. When it comes to solving the problems of everyday living, we often know precisely what needs to be done, but we may be slow in doing it—especially if what needs to be done is difficult. So we put off till tomorrow what should be done today.

As a young person, you have your own set of challenges. As you face those challenges, you may be comforted by this fact: Trouble, of every kind, is temporary. Yet God's grace is eternal. And worries, of every kind, are temporary. But God's love is everlasting. The troubles that concern you will pass. God remains. And for every problem, God has a solution.

The words of Psalm 34 remind us that the Lord solves problems for "people who do what is right." And usually, doing "what is right" means doing the uncomfortable work of confronting our problems sooner rather than later. So with no further ado, let the problem-solving begin . . . right now.

Each problem is a God-appointed instructor.

Charles Swindoll

Hope looks for the good in people, opens doors for people, discovers what can be done to help, lights a candle, does not yield to cynicism. Hope sets people free.

Barbara Johnson

TODAY'S PRAYER

Dear Lord, the things that seem like problems to me may actually be opportunities from You. So today, I will focus, not on the challenges I face, but on the opportunities I've been given. Amen

GOD'S TIMETABLE

He has made everything appropriate in its time.
He has also put eternity in their hearts,
but man cannot discover the work
God has done from beginning to end.

Ecclesiastes 3:11 HCSB

Are you anxious for God to work out His plan for your life? Who isn't? As believers, we all want God to do great things for us and through us, and we want Him to do those things now. But sometimes, God has other plans. Sometimes, God's timetable does not coincide with our own. It's worth noting, however, that God's timetable is always perfect.

The next time you find your patience tested to the limit, remember that the world unfolds according to God's plan, not ours. Sometimes, we must wait patiently, and that's as it should be. After all, think about how patient God has been with us.

Will not the Lord's time be better than your time?

C. H. Spurgeon

God has a designated time when his promise will be fulfilled and the prayer will be answered.

Jim Cymbala

When there is perplexity there is always guidance—not always at the moment we ask, but in good time, which is God's time. There is no need to fret and stew.

Elisabeth Elliot

Your times are in His hands. He's in charge of the timetable, so wait patiently.

Kay Arthur

TODAY'S PRAYER

Lord, my sense of timing is fallible and imperfect; Yours is not. Let me trust in Your timetable for my life, and give me the patience and the wisdom to trust Your plans, not my own. Amen

THE CHOICE TO AVOID GOSSIP

So rid yourselves of all wickedness, all deceit, hypocrisy, envy, and all slander.

1 Peter 2:1 HCSB

Face facts: gossip is the guilty little pleasure that tempts almost all of us from time to time. Why is it so tempting to gossip? Because when we put other people down, we experience a brief dose of self-righteousness as we look down our noses at the misdeeds of others. But there's a catch: in truth, we can never really build ourselves up by tearing other people down. So the habit of gossip turns out to be a self-defeating waste of time.

It's no wonder that the Bible clearly teaches that gossip is wrong. Consider the simple advice found in Proverbs 16:28: "Gossip ruins friendships" (NCV). So do yourself a big favor: don't spend precious time talking about other people. It's a waste of words, it's the wrong thing to do, and in the end, it will leave you with less self-respect, not more.

When you avoid the temptation to engage in gossip, you'll feel better about yourself—and other people will feel better about you, too. So don't do it.

Change the heart, and you change the speech.

Warren Wiersbe

The great test of a man's character is his tongue.

Oswald Chambers

The cost of gossip always exceeds its worth.

Marie T. Freeman

TODAY'S PRAYER

Dear Lord, it's tempting to gossip, but it's wrong. Today and every day, help me speak words that are pleasing to You, and help me treat other people in the same way that I want to be treated by them. Amen

145

FORM HABITS THAT ARE PLEASING TO GOD

I, the Lord, examine the mind,
I test the heart to give to each according to his way,
according to what his actions deserve.
Jeremiah 17:10 HCSB

It's an old saying and a true one: First, you make your habits, and then your habits make you. Some habits will inevitably bring you closer to God; other habits will lead you away from the path He has chosen for you. If you sincerely desire to improve your spiritual health, you must honestly examine the habits that make up the fabric of your day. And you must abandon those habits that are displeasing to God.

If you trust God, and if you keep asking for His help, He can transform your life. If you sincerely ask Him to help you, the same God who created the universe will help you defeat the harmful habits that have heretofore defeated you. So, if at first you don't succeed, keep praying. God is listening, and He's ready to help you become a better person if you ask Him . . . so ask today.

You can build up a set of good habits so that you habitually take the Christian way without thought.

E. Stanley Jones

You will never change your life until you change something you do daily.

John Maxwell

TODAY'S PRAYER

Dear Lord, help me break bad habits and form good ones. And let my actions be pleasing to You, today, tomorrow, and every day of my life. Amen

147

HOLINESS BEFORE HAPPINESS

Blessed are those who hunger and thirst for righteousness, because they will be filled.

Matthew 5:6 HCSB

Because you are an imperfect human being, you are not "perfectly" happy—and that's perfectly okay with God. He is far less concerned with your happiness than He is with your holiness.

God continuously reveals Himself in everyday life, but He does not do so in order to make you contented; He does so in order to lead you to His Son. So don't be overly concerned with your current level of happiness; it will change. Be more concerned with the current state of your relationship with Christ: He does not change. And because your Savior transcends time and space, you can be comforted in the knowledge that in the end, His joy will become your joy . . . for all eternity.

You don't have to be like the world to have an impact on the world. You don't have to be like the crowd to change the crowd. You don't have to lower yourself down to their level to lift them up to your level. Holiness doesn't seek to be odd. Holiness seeks to be like God.

Max Lucado

A holy life simply is a life that works.

Richard Foster

Our ultimate aim in life is not to be healthy, wealthy, prosperous, or problem free. Our ultimate aim in life is to bring glory to God.

Anne Graham Lotz

TODAY'S PRAYER

Lord, Your laws are perfect; let me live by those laws. And, let my life be a testimony to the power of righteousness and to the wisdom of Your commandments. Amen

BE CAREFUL HOW YOU DIRECT YOUR THOUGHTS

Be careful what you think,
because your thoughts run your life.
Proverbs 4:23 NCV

How will you direct your thoughts today? Will you obey the words of Philippians 4:8 by dwelling upon those things that are honorable, true, and worthy of praise? Or will you allow your thoughts to be hijacked by the negativity that seems to dominate our troubled world?

Are you fearful, angry, bored, or worried? Are you so preoccupied with the concerns of this day that you fail to thank God for the promise of eternity? Are you confused or pessimistic? If so, God wants to have a little talk with you. He wants to remind you of His infinite love and His boundless grace. As you contemplate these things, and as you give thanks for God's blessings, negativity should no longer dominate your day or your life.

Our own possible bad thoughts and deeds are far more dangerous to us than any enemy from the world.

St. Ambrose

People who do not develop and practice good thinking often find themselves at the mercy of their circumstances.

John Maxwell

I became aware of one very important concept I had missed before: my attitude—not my circumstances—was what was making me unhappy.

Vonette Bright

TODAY'S PRAYER

Dear Lord, let my thoughts and prayers honor You. When I become fearful or discouraged, let me trust You. And when I encounter the evils of this world, let me turn to You for strength and wisdom. Amen

151

TRUSTING GOD

It is better to trust the Lord than to put confidence in people. It is better to trust the Lord than to put confidence in princes.

Psalm 118:8-9 NLT

Sometimes the future seems bright, and sometimes it does not. Yet even when we cannot see the possibilities of tomorrow, God can. As believers, our challenge is to trust an uncertain future to an all-powerful God.

When we trust God, we should trust Him without reservation. We should steel ourselves against the inevitable stresses of the day, secure in the knowledge that our Heavenly Father has a plan for the future that only He can see.

Can you place your future into the hands of a loving and all-knowing God? Can you live amid the uncertainties of today, knowing that God has dominion over all your tomorrows? If you can, you are wise and you are blessed. When you trust God with everything you are and everything you have, He will bless you now and forever.

Conditions are always changing; therefore, I must not be dependent upon conditions. What matters supremely is my soul and my relationship to God.

Corrie ten Boom

True faith is man's weakness leaning on God's strength.

D. L. Moody

Sometimes the very essence of faith is trusting God in the midst of things He knows good and well we cannot comprehend.

Beth Moore

TODAY'S PRAYER

Dear Lord, as I take the next steps on my life's journey, let me take them with You. Whatever the coming day may bring, I will thank You for the opportunity to live abundantly. I will be Your faithful, faith-filled servant, Lord—and I will trust You—this day and forever. Amen

153

WHAT TO DO ABOUT EVIL

Take your stand with God's loyal community and live, or chase after phantoms of evil and die.
Proverbs 11:19 MSG

The better you get to know God, the more you'll understand how God wants you to respond to evil. And make no mistake, this world is inhabited by quite a few people who are very determined to do evil things. The devil and his human helpers are working 24/7 to cause pain and heartbreak in every corner of the globe . . . including your corner. So you'd better beware.

Your job, if you choose to accept it, is to recognize evil and fight it. The moment that you decide to fight evil whenever you see it, you can no longer be a lukewarm, halfhearted Christian.

When will you choose to get serious about fighting the evils of our world? Before you answer that question, consider this: in the battle of good versus evil, the devil never takes a day off . . . and neither should you.

Rebuke the Enemy in your own name and he laughs; command him in the name of Christ and he flees.

John Eldredge

He who passively accepts evil is as much involved in it as he who helps to perpetrate it. He who accepts evil without protesting against it is really cooperating with it.

Martin Luther King, Jr.

God loves you, and He yearns for you to turn away from the path of evil. You need His forgiveness, and you need Him to come into your life and remake you from within.

Billy Graham

TODAY'S PRAYER

Dear Lord, give me the wisdom to recognize evil and the courage to fight it, today and every day of my life. Amen

WHAT A FRIEND

Therefore if any man be in Christ, he is a new creature: old things are passed away; behold, all things are become new.

2 Corinthians 5:17 KJV

Our circumstances change but Jesus does not. Even when the world seems to be trembling between our feet, Jesus remains the spiritual bedrock that cannot be moved.

The old familiar hymn begins, "What a friend we have in Jesus . . . ." No truer words were ever penned. Jesus is the sovereign Friend and ultimate Savior of mankind. Christ showed enduring love for His believers by willingly sacrificing His own life so that we might have eternal life. Let us love Him, praise Him, and share His message of salvation with our neighbors and with the world.

Jesus was the perfect reflection of God's nature in every situation He encountered during His time here on earth.

Bill Hybels

Jesus: the proof of God's love.

Philip Yancey

Our responsibility is to feed from Him, to stay close to Him, to follow Him—because sheep easily go astray—so that we eternally experience the protection and companionship of our Great Shepherd the Lord Jesus Christ.

Franklin Graham

TODAY'S PRAYER

Heavenly Father, I praise You for Your Son. Jesus is my Savior and my strength. Let me share His Good News with all who cross my path, and let me share His love with all who need His healing touch. Amen

157

MAKE CHRIST YOUR FOCUS

Then Jesus spoke to them again: "I am the light of the world. Anyone who follows Me will never walk in the darkness, but will have the light of life."

John 8:12 HCSB

Is Christ the focus of your life? Are you fired with enthusiasm for Him? Are you an energized Christian who allows God's Son to reign over every aspect of your day? Make no mistake: that's exactly what God intends for you to do.

God has given you the gift of eternal life through His Son. In response to God's priceless gift, you are instructed to focus your thoughts, your prayers, and your energies upon God and His only begotten Son. To do so, you must resist the subtle yet powerful temptation to become a "spiritual dabbler."

A person who dabbles in the Christian faith is unwilling to place God in His rightful place: above all other things. Resist that temptation;

make God the cornerstone and the touchstone of your life. When you do, He will give you all the strength and wisdom you need to live victoriously for Him.

I am truly happy with Jesus Christ. I couldn't live without Him. When my life gets beyond the ability to cope, He takes over.

Ruth Bell Graham

Whatever is your best time in the day, give that to communion with God.

Hudson Taylor

TODAY'S PRAYER

Lord, You sent Your Son so that I might have a life that is abundant and eternal. Thank You, Lord, for Jesus, for His sacrifices, and for His love. Because Jesus is my Savior, I am blessed by His grace forever. Amen

DECIDING NOT TO BE JUDGMENTAL

Stop judging others, and you will not be judged.
Stop criticizing others, or it will all
come back on you. If you forgive others,
you will be forgiven.
Luke 6:37 NLT

Here's something worth thinking about: If you judge other people harshly, God will judge you in the same fashion. But that's not all (thank goodness!). The Bible also promises that if you forgive others, you, too, will be forgiven. Have you developed the bad habit of behaving yourself like an amateur judge and jury, assigning blame and condemnation wherever you go? If so, it's time to grow up and obey God. When it comes to judging everything and everybody, God doesn't need your help . . . and He doesn't want it.

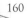

Christians think they are prosecuting attorneys or judges, when, in reality, God has called all of us to be witnesses.

Warren Wiersbe

It is time that the followers of Jesus revise their language and learn to speak respectfully of non-Christian peoples.

Lottie Moon

Jesus lives in the community; He only visits the church.

Anonymous

TODAY'S PRAYER

Lord, it's so easy to judge other people, but it's also easy to misjudge them. Only You can judge a human heart, Lord, so let me love my friends and neighbors, and let me help them, but never let me judge them. Amen

BE KIND TO EVERYBODY

And be kind and compassionate to one another,
forgiving one another,
just as God also forgave you in Christ.

Ephesians 4:32 HCSB

Would you like an ironclad formula for improved self-esteem? Try this: be kind to everybody.

Kindness is a choice. Sometimes, when you feel happy or generous, you may find it easy to be kind. Other times, when you are discouraged or tired, you can scarcely summon the energy to utter a single kind word. But, God's commandment is clear: He intends that you make the conscious choice to treat others with kindness and respect, no matter your circumstances, no matter your emotions.

So today, spread a heaping helping of kindness wherever you go. When you do, you'll discover that the more kindness you give away to others, the more you'll receive in return.

A little kindly advice is better than a great deal of scolding.

Fanny Crosby

When you launch an act of kindness out into the crosswinds of life, it will blow kindness back to you.

Dennis Swanberg

Do all the good you can. By all the means you can. In all the ways you can. In all the places you can. At all the times you can. To all the people you can. As long as ever you can.

John Wesley

TODAY'S PRAYER

Lord, it's easy to be kind to some people and difficult to be kind to others. Let me be kind to all people so that I might follow in the footsteps of Your Son. Amen

163

KEEP LEARNING EVERY DAY

It takes knowledge to fill a home with rare and beautiful treasures.

Proverbs 24:4 NCV

Another way to feel better about yourself is to keep acquiring both knowledge and wisdom. Knowledge is found in textbooks. Wisdom, on the other hand, is found in God's Holy Word and in the carefully-chosen words of loving parents, family members, and friends.

Knowledge is an important building block in a well-lived life, and it pays rich dividends both personally and professionally. But, wisdom is even more important because it refashions not only the mind, but also the heart.

When you study God's Word and live according to His commandments, you will become wise . . . and you will be a blessing to your family and to the world.

While chastening is always difficult, if we look to God for the lesson we should learn, we will see spiritual fruit.

Vonette Bright

The wonderful thing about God's schoolroom is that we get to grade our own papers. You see, He doesn't test us so He can learn how well we're doing. He tests us so we can discover how well we're doing.

Charles Swindoll

It's the things you learn after you know it all that really count.

Vance Havner

TODAY'S PRAYER

Dear Lord, I have so much to learn. Help me to watch, to listen, to think, and to learn, every day of my life. Amen

165

IT'S A WONDERFUL LIFE

*For whoever finds me finds life
and receives favor from the LORD.*
Proverbs 8:35 NIV

Life can be tough sometimes, but it's also wonderful—and it's a glorious gift from God. How will you use that gift? Every day, including this one, comes gift-wrapped from God—your job is to unwrap that gift, to use it wisely, and to give thanks to the Giver.

Instead of sleepwalking through life, you must wake up and live in the precious present. Each waking moment holds the potential to celebrate, to serve, to share, or to love. Because you are a person with incalculable potential, each moment has incalculable value. Your challenge is to experience each day to the fullest as you seek to live in accordance with God's plan for your life. When you do, you'll experience His abundance and His peace.

Are you willing to treat this day (and every one hereafter) as a special gift to be savored and celebrated? You should—and if you seek to Live with a capital L, you most certainly will.

People, places, and things were never meant to give us life. God alone is the author of a fulfilling life.

Gary Smalley & John Trent

The Christian life is motivated, not by a list of do's and don'ts, but by the gracious outpouring of God's love and blessing.

Anne Graham Lotz

TODAY'S PRAYER

Lord, You have given me the gift of life. Let me treasure it, and let me use it for Your service and for Your glory. Amen

LISTENING TO GOD

The one who is from God listens to God's words.
This is why you don't listen,
because you are not from God.
John 8:47 HCSB

Sometimes God speaks loudly and clearly. More often, He speaks in a quiet voice—and if you are wise, you will be listening carefully when He does. To do so, you must carve out quiet moments each day to study His Word and sense His direction.

Can you quiet yourself long enough to listen to your conscience? Are you attuned to the subtle guidance of your intuition? Are you willing to pray sincerely and then to wait quietly for God's response? Hopefully so. Usually God refrains from sending His messages on stone tablets or city billboards. More often, He communicates in subtler ways. If you sincerely desire to hear His voice, you must listen carefully, and you must do so in the silent corners of your quiet, willing heart.

When we come to Jesus stripped of pretensions, with a needy spirit, ready to listen, He meets us at the point of need.

Catherine Marshall

God is always listening.

Stormie Omartian

Listening is loving.

Zig Ziglar

In the soul-searching of our lives, we are to stay quiet so we can hear Him say all that He wants to say to us in our hearts.

Charles Swindoll

TODAY'S PRAYER

Dear Lord, I have so much to learn and You have so much to teach me. Give me the wisdom to be still and the discernment to hear Your voice, today and every day. Amen

DON'T OVERESTIMATE THE IMPORTANCE OF STUFF

And He told them, "Watch out and be on guard against all greed, because one's life is not in the abundance of his possessions."
Luke 12:15 HCSB

How important are our material possessions? Not as important as we might think. In a well-balanced life, material possessions should play a rather small role. Of course, we all need the basic necessities of life, but once we meet those needs for ourselves and for our families, the piling up of possessions often creates more problems than it solves. Our real riches are not of this world. We are never really rich until we are rich in spirit.

If you've become preoccupied with money and the things that money can buy, it's time to de-emphasize material things and re-emphasize spiritual things. When you do, you'll feel better about yourself . . . and you'll begin storing up riches that will endure forever: the spiritual kind.

A society that pursues pleasure runs the risk of raising expectations ever higher, so that true contentment always lies tantalizingly out of reach.

Philip Yancey and Paul Brand

It's sobering to contemplate how much time, effort, sacrifice, compromise, and attention we give to acquiring and increasing our supply of something that is totally insignificant in eternity.

Anne Graham Lotz

When possessions become our god, we become materialistic and greedy . . . and we forfeit our contentment and our joy.

Charles Swindoll

TODAY'S PRAYER

Dear Lord, help me remember that the things in this world that are really valuable are my life, my family, and my relationship with You. Amen

REMEMBER THAT ACTIONS SPEAK LOUDER

For the kingdom of God is not in talk but in power.
1 Corinthians 4:20 HCSB

The old saying is both familiar and true: actions speak louder than words. And as believers, we must beware: our actions should always give credence to the changes that Christ can make in the lives of those who walk with Him.

God calls upon each of us to act in accordance with His will and with respect for His commandments. If we are to be responsible believers, we must realize that it is never enough simply to hear the instructions of God; we must also live by them. And it is never enough to wait idly by while others do God's work here on earth; we, too, must act. Doing God's work is a responsibility that each of us must bear, and when we do, our loving Heavenly Father rewards our efforts with a bountiful harvest.

Every word we speak, every action we take, has an effect on the totality of humanity. No one can escape that privilege—or that responsibility.

Laurie Beth Jones

It is by acts and not by ideas that people live.

Harry Emerson Fosdick

Never fail to do something because you don't feel like it. Sometimes you just have to do it now, and you'll feel like it later.

Marie T. Freeman

TODAY'S PRAYER

Dear Lord, I have heard Your Word, and I have felt Your presence in my heart; let me act accordingly. Let my words and actions show people the changes You have made in my life. Let me praise You, Father, by following in the footsteps of Your Son, and let others see Him through me. Amen

173

MAKE THE MOST OF YOUR TALENTS

Do not neglect the gift that is in you.
1 Timothy 4:14 HCSB

Face it: you've got an array of talents that need to be refined—and you'll feel better about yourself when you refine them. But nobody will force you to do the hard work of converting raw talent into prime-time talent. That's a job you must do for yourself.

Today, make a promise to yourself that you will earnestly seek to discover the talents that God has given you. Then, nourish those talents and make them grow. Finally, vow to share your gifts with the world for as long as God gives you the power to do so. When you do, you'll feel better about yourself and your abilities . . . and the world will, too.

Employ whatever God has entrusted you with, in doing good, all possible good, in every possible kind and degree.

John Wesley

God often reveals His direction for our lives through the way He made us…with a certain personality and unique skills.

Bill Hybels

If you want to reach your potential, you need to add a strong work ethic to your talent.

John Maxwell

You are the only person on earth who can use your ability.

Zig Ziglar

TODAY'S PRAYER

Lord, You gave me talents and abilities for a reason. Let me use my talents for the glory of Your kingdom, and let me praise You always because You are the Giver of all gifts, including mine. Amen

175

WHO WILL YOU FOLLOW?

"Follow Me," Jesus told them,
"and I will make you into fishers of men!"
Immediately they left their nets and followed Him.
Mark 1:17-18 HCSB

Can you honestly say that you're passionate about your faith and that you're really following Jesus? Hopefully so. But if you're preoccupied with other things—or if you're strictly a one-day-a-week Christian—then you're in need of a major-league spiritual makeover.

Jesus doesn't want you to be a lukewarm believer; Jesus wants you to be a "new creation" through Him. And that's exactly what you should want for yourself, too. Nothing is more important than your wholehearted commitment to your Creator and to His only begotten Son. Your faith must never be an afterthought; it must be your ultimate priority, your ultimate possession, and your ultimate passion.

You are the recipient of Christ's love. Accept it enthusiastically and share it passionately. Jesus deserves your undivided attention. And when you give it to Him, you'll be forever grateful that you did.

Jesus challenges you and me to keep our focus daily on the cross of His will if we want to be His disciples.

Anne Graham Lotz

It's your heart that Jesus longs for: your will to be made His own with self on the cross forever, and Jesus alone on the throne.

Ruth Bell Graham

TODAY'S PRAYER

Dear Lord, You sent Jesus to save the world and to save me. I thank You for Jesus, and I will do my best to follow Him, today and forever. Amen

THE DECISION TO WORSHIP GOD EVERY DAY

Worship the Lord your God and . . .
serve Him only.
Matthew 4:10 HCSB

If you really want to know God, you must be willing to worship Him seven days a week, not just on Sunday.

God has a wonderful plan for your life, and an important part of that plan includes the time that you set aside for praise and worship. Every life, including yours, is based upon some form of worship. The question is not whether you will worship, but what you worship.

If you choose to worship God, you will receive a bountiful harvest of joy, peace, and abundance. But if you distance yourself from God by foolishly worshiping earthly possessions and personal gratification, you're making a huge mistake. So do this: Worship God today and every day. Worship

Him with sincerity and thanksgiving. Write His name on your heart and rest assured that He, too, has written your name on His.

Worship is a voluntary act of gratitude offered by the saved to the Savior, by the healed to the Healer, by the delivered to the Deliverer.

Max Lucado

To worship Him in truth means to worship Him honestly, without hypocrisy, standing open and transparent before Him.

Anne Graham Lotz

TODAY'S PRAYER

Lord, when I slow down and take the time to worship You, my soul is blessed. Let me worship You every day of my life, and let me discover the peace that can be mine when I welcome You into my heart. Amen

EXCUSES EVERYWHERE

People's own foolishness ruins their lives,
but in their minds they blame the Lord.

Proverbs 19:3 NCV

Excuses are everywhere . . . excellence is not. Whether you're a student or a corporate CEO, your work is a picture book of your priorities. So whatever your job description, it's up to you, and no one else, to become masterful at your craft. It's up to you to do your job right, and to do it right now.

Because we humans are such creative excuse-makers, all of the best excuses have already been taken—we've heard them all before.

So if you're wasting your time trying to concoct a new and improved excuse, don't bother. It's impossible. A far better strategy is this: do the work. Now. Then, let your excellent work speak loudly and convincingly for itself.

An excuse is only the skin of a reason stuffed with a lie.

Vance Havner

We need to stop focusing on our lacks and stop giving out excuses and start looking at and listening to Jesus.

Anne Graham Lotz

Making up a string of excuses is usually harder than doing the work.

Marie T. Freeman

TODAY'S PRAYER

Heavenly Father, how easy it is to make excuses. But, I want to be a person who accomplishes important work for You. Help me, Father, to strive for excellence, not excuses. Amen

THE RIGHT KIND OF FELLOWSHIP

So reach out and welcome one another to
God's glory. Jesus did it; now you do it!
Romans 15:7 MSG

If you genuinely want to become the kind of person who experiences a closer relationship with God, you'll need to build closer relationships with godly people. That's why fellowship with like-minded believers should be an integral part of your life. Your association with fellow Christians should be uplifting, enlightening, encouraging, and (above all) consistent.

Are your friends the kind of people who encourage you to seek God's will and to obey God's Word? If so, you've chosen your friends wisely. And that's a good thing because when you choose friends who honor God, you'll find it easier to honor Him, too.

One of the ways God refills us after failure is through the blessing of Christian fellowship. Just experiencing the joy of simple activities shared with other children of God can have a healing effect on us.

Anne Graham Lotz

I hope you will find a few folks who walk with God to also walk with you through the seasons of your life.

John Eldredge

Real fellowship happens when people get honest about who they are and what is happening in their lives.

Rick Warren

TODAY'S PRAYER

Heavenly Father, You have given me a community of supporters called the church. Let our fellowship be a reflection of the love we feel for each other and the love we feel for You. Amen

183

BEYOND FEAR

*I sought the Lord, and He answered me and
delivered me from all my fears.*

Psalm 34:4 HCSB

We live in a world that is, at times, a frightening place. We live in a world that is, at times, a discouraging place. We live in a world where life-changing losses can be so painful and so profound that it seems we will never recover. But, with God's help, and with the help of encouraging family members and friends, we can recover.

During the darker days of life, we are wise to remember the words of Jesus, who reassured His disciples, saying, "Take courage! It is I. Don't be afraid" (Matthew 14:27 NIV). Then, with God's comfort and His love in our hearts, we can offer encouragement to others. And by helping them face their fears, we can, in turn, tackle our own problems with courage, determination, and faith.

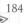

The Lord Jesus by His Holy Spirit is with me, and the knowledge of His presence dispels the darkness and allays any fears.

Bill Bright

When we meditate on God and remember the promises He has given us in His Word, our faith grows, and our fears dissolve.

Charles Stanley

When once we are assured that God is good, then there can be nothing left to fear.

Hannah Whitall Smith

TODAY'S PRAYER

Dear Lord, when I am fearful, keep me mindful that You are my protector and my salvation. Thank You, Father, for a perfect love that casts out fear. Because of You, I can live courageously and faithfully this day and every day. Amen

DO FIRST THINGS FIRST

Therefore, get your minds ready for action,
being self-disciplined . . . .
1 Peter 1:13 HCSB

"First things first." These words are easy to speak but hard to put into practice. For busy people living in a demanding world, placing first things first can be difficult indeed. Why? Because so many people are expecting so many things from us!

If you're having trouble prioritizing your day, perhaps you've been trying to organize your life according to your own plans, not God's. A better strategy, of course, is to take your daily obligations and place them in the hands of the One who created you. To do so, you must prioritize your day according to God's commandments, and you must seek His will and His wisdom in all matters. Then, you can face the day with the assurance that the same God who created our universe out of nothingness will help you place first things first in your own life.

Do you feel overwhelmed or confused? Turn the concerns of this day over to God—prayerfully, earnestly, and often. Then, listen for His answer . . . and trust the answer He gives.

Blessed are those who know what on earth they are here on earth to do and set themselves about the business of doing it.

Max Lucado

No test of a man's true character is more conclusive than how he spends his time and his money.

Patrick Morley

TODAY'S PRAYER

Dear Lord, today is a new day. Help me finish the important tasks first, even if those tasks are unpleasant. Give me the wisdom and the courage to do what needs to be done, when it needs to be done . . . and let me teach others to do the same. Amen

TEMPTATIONS ARE EVERYWHERE

Put on the whole armor of God, that you may be able to stand against the wiles of the devil.

Ephesians 6:11 NKJV

Face facts: you live a temptation-filled world. The devil is working hard in your neighborhood, and so are his helpers. Here in the 21st century, the bad guys are working around the clock to lead you astray. That's why you must remain vigilant.

In a letter to believers, Peter offers a stern warning: "Your adversary, the devil, prowls around like a roaring lion, seeking someone to devour" (1 Peter 5:8 NASB). What was true in New Testament times is equally true in our own. Satan tempts his prey and then devours them.

As a believer who seeks a radical relationship with Jesus, you must beware because temptations are everywhere. Satan is determined to win; you must be equally determined that he does not.

Jesus faced every temptation known to humanity so that He could identify with us.

Beth Moore

Our battles are first won or lost in the secret places of our will in God's presence, never in full view of the world.

Oswald Chambers

Flee temptation without leaving a forwarding address.

Barbara Johnson

Temptation is not a sin. Even Jesus was tempted. The Lord Jesus gives you the strength needed to resist temptation.

Corrie ten Boom

TODAY'S PRAYER

Lord, temptation is everywhere! Help me turn from it and to run from it! Let me keep Christ in my heart, and let me put the devil in his place: far away from me! Amen

FORGIVE:
IT'S GOD'S WAY

You have heard that it was said,
You shall love your neighbor and hate your enemy.
But I tell you, love your enemies,
and pray for those who persecute you.
Matthew 5:43-44 HCSB

It has been said that life is an exercise in forgiveness. How true. Christ understood the importance of forgiveness when he commanded, "Love your enemies and pray for those who persecute you" (Matthew 5:43-44 NIV). But sometimes, forgiveness is difficult indeed.

When we have been injured or embarrassed, we feel the urge to strike back and to hurt the one who has hurt us. Christ instructs us to do otherwise. Believers are taught that forgiveness is God's way and that mercy is an integral part of God's plan for our lives. In short, we are commanded to weave the thread of forgiveness into the very fabric of our lives.

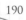

Today, as you go about your daily affairs, remember that you have already been forgiven by your Heavenly Father, and so, too, should you forgive others. If you bear bitterness against anyone, take your bitterness to God and leave it there. If you are angry, pray for God's healing hand to calm your spirit. If you are troubled by some past injustice, read God's Word and remember His commandment to forgive. When you follow that commandment and sincerely forgive those who have hurt you, you'll discover that a heavy burden has been lifted from your shoulders. And, you'll discover that although forgiveness is indeed difficult, with God's help, all things are possible.

TODAY'S PRAYER

Lord, just as You have forgiven me, I am going to forgive others. When I forgive others, I not only obey Your commandments, but I also free myself from bitterness and regret. Forgiveness is Your way, Lord, and I will make it my way, too. Amen

191

DON'T UNDERESTIMATE THE IMPORTANCE OF YOUR FRIENDS

As iron sharpens iron, a friend sharpens a friend.

Proverbs 27:17 NLT

When you hang out with positive people, you feel better about yourself and your world—when you hang out with negative people, you won't. So here's the question: do you want to feel better about yourself and your circumstances . . . or not? The answer you give should help you determine the friends you choose to make—and keep.

If you're really serious about being an optimistic, upbeat, hope-filled Christian, make sure that your friends feel the same way. Because if you choose to hang out with upbeat people, you'll tend to be an upbeat person, too. But if you hang out with the critics, the cynics, and the naysayers, you'll find yourself become a cynic, too. And life is far too short for that.

The next best thing to being wise oneself is to live in a circle of those who are.

C. S. Lewis

For better or worse, you will eventually become more and more like the people you associate with. So why not associate with people who make you better, not worse?

Marie T. Freeman

Yes, the Spirit was sent to be our Counselor. Yes, Jesus speaks to us personally. But often he works through another human being.

John Eldredge

A friend is one who makes me do my best.

Oswald Chambers

TODAY'S PRAYER

Thank You, Lord, for my friends, the people who enrich my life. I pray for them today, and ask Your blessings upon them . . . and upon me. Amen

TREAT ADDICTIVE SUBSTANCES LIKE POISON

*Be sober! Be on the alert! Your adversary
the Devil is prowling around like a roaring lion,
looking for anyone he can devour.*

1 Peter 5:8 HCSB

If you'd like a perfect formula for low (or no) self-respect, here it is: get addicted to something that destroys your health or your sanity. If (God forbid) you allow yourself to become addicted, you're steering straight for a boatload of negative consequences, not to mention a big bad dose of negative self-esteem.

Unless you're living on a deserted island, you know people who are full-blown addicts—probably lots of people. If you, or someone you love, is suffering from the blight of addiction, remember this: Help is available. Plenty of people have experienced addiction and lived to tell about it . . . so don't give up hope.

And if you're one of those fortunate people who hasn't started experimenting with addictive substances, congratulations! You have just spared yourself a lifetime of headaches and heartaches.

A man may not be responsible for his last drink, but he certainly was for the first.

Billy Graham

The soul that journeys to God, but doesn't shake off its cares and quiet its appetites, is like someone who drags a cart uphill.

St. John of the Cross

TODAY'S PRAYER

Dear Lord, You have instructed me to care for my body, and I will obey You. I will be mindful of the destructive power of addiction, and I will avoid the people, the places, and the substances that can entrap my spirit and destroy my life. Amen

SERVE HIM

The greatest among you will be your servant.
Whoever exalts himself will be humbled, and
whoever humbles himself will be exalted.
Matthew 23:11-12 HCSB

We live in a world that glorifies power, prestige, fame, and money. But the words of Jesus teach us that the most esteemed men and women in this world are not the self-congratulatory leaders of society but are instead the humblest of servants.

Are you willing to become a humble servant for Christ? Are you willing to pitch in and make the world a better place, or are you determined to keep all your blessings to yourself. The answers to these questions will determine the quality and the direction of your day and your life.

Today, you may feel the temptation to take more than you give. You may be tempted to with-hold your generosity. Or you may be tempted to build yourself up in the eyes of your friends. Resist those temptations. Instead, serve your friends quietly and without fanfare. Find a need and fill it . . . humbly. Lend a helping hand . . . anonymously. Share a word of kindness . . . with quiet sincerity. As you go about your daily activities, remember that the Savior of all humanity made Himself a servant, and we, as His followers, must do no less.

God wants us to serve Him with a willing spirit, one that would choose no other way.

Beth Moore

Through our service to others, God wants to influence our world for Him.

Vonette Bright

TODAY'S PRAYER

Dear Lord, let me help others in every way that I can. Jesus served others; I can too. I will serve other people with my good deeds and with my prayers. And I will give thanks for everybody who helps me. Amen

A LITTLE SILENCE

*Be silent before the Lord and wait
expectantly for Him.*
Psalm 37:7 HCSB

When you have doubts, remember this: God isn't on a coffee break, and He hasn't moved out of town. God isn't taking a long vacation, and He isn't snoozing on the couch. He's right here, right now, listening to your thoughts and prayers, watching over your every move.

The Bible teaches that a wonderful way to get to know God is simply to be still and listen to Him. But sometimes, you may find it hard to slow down and listen. As the demands of everyday life weigh down upon you, you may be tempted to ignore God's presence or—worse yet—to rebel against His commandments. But, when you quiet yourself and acknowledge His presence, God touches your heart and restores your spirits. So why not let Him do it right now? If you really want to know Him better, silence is a wonderful place to start.

Growth takes place in quietness, in hidden ways, in silence and solitude. The process is not accessible to observation.

Eugene Peterson

If you, too, will learn to wait upon God, to get alone with Him, and remain silent so that you can hear His voice when He is ready to speak to you, what a difference it will make in your life!

Kay Arthur

There are times when to speak is to violate the moment—when silence represents the highest respect. The word for such times is reverence.

Max Lucado

TODAY'S PRAYER

Dear Lord, life is complicated enough without my adding to the confusion. Help me understand the wisdom of simplicity. Wherever I happen to be, help me to keep it simple—very simple. Amen

HAVE A HEALTHY FEAR OF GOD

Since we are receiving a Kingdom that cannot be destroyed, let us be thankful and please God by worshiping him with holy fear and awe.

Hebrews 12:28 NLT

Do you possess a healthy, fearful respect for God's power? Hopefully so. After all, the lesson from the Book of Proverbs is clear: "The fear of the Lord is the beginning of knowledge, but fools despise wisdom and instruction" (1:7 NKJV). Yet, you live in a world that often ignores the role that God plays in shaping the affairs of mankind. You live in a world where too many people consider it "unfashionable" or "unseemly" to discuss the fear of God. Don't count yourself among their number.

God maintains absolute sovereignty over His creation, and His power is beyond comprehension. As believers, we must cultivate a sincere respect for God's awesome power. The fear of the

Lord is, indeed, the beginning of knowledge. So today, as you face the realities of everyday life, remember this: until you acquire a healthy, respectful fear of God's power, your education is incomplete, and so is your faith.

A healthy fear of God will do much to deter us from sin.

Charles Swindoll

The remarkable thing about fearing God is that when you fear God, you fear nothing else, whereas if you do not fear God, you fear everything else.

Oswald Chambers

TODAY'S PRAYER

Lord, You love me and protect me. I praise You, Father, for Your grace, and I respect You for Your infinite power. Let my greatest fear in life be the fear of displeasing You. Amen

REMEMBER THAT SIN ENSLAVES

Jesus responded, "I assure you:
Everyone who commits sin is a slave of sin."
John 8:34 HCSB

Because we are creatures of free will, we may disobey God whenever we choose. But when we do so, we put ourselves and our loved ones in peril. Why? Because disobedience invites disaster. We cannot sin against God without consequences. We cannot live outside His will without injury. We cannot distance ourselves from God without hardening our hearts. We cannot yield to the ever-tempting distractions of our world and, at the same time, enjoy God's peace.

Sometimes, in a futile attempt to justify our behaviors, we make a distinction between "big" sins and "little" ones. To do so is a mistake of "big" proportions. Sins of all shapes and sizes have the power to do us great harm. And in a world where sin is big business, that's certainly a sobering thought.

Before we can be filled with the Living Water, we must be cleansed of sin. Before we can be cleansed of sin, we must be convicted. And sometimes it's painful. And shameful.

Anne Graham Lotz

We cannot out-sin God's ability to forgive us.

Beth Moore

He loved us even while we were yet sinners at war with Him!

Bill Bright

There's none so blind as those who will not see.

Matthew Henry

TODAY'S PRAYER

Dear Lord, when I make mistakes, You forgive me. Thank You, Lord, for Your love, for Your forgiveness, and for Your Son. Amen

203

SHARE YOUR FAITH

And I say to you, anyone who acknowledges Me before men, the Son of Man will also acknowledge him before the angels of God; but whoever denies Me before men will be denied before the angels of God.

Luke 12:8-9 HCSB

Let's get one thing straight: those of us who are Christians should be willing to talk about the things that Christ has done for us. Our personal testimonies are vitally important, but sometimes, because of shyness or insecurities, we're afraid to share our experiences. And that's unfortunate.

We live in a world that desperately needs the healing message of Christ Jesus. Every believer, each in his or her own way, bears responsibility for sharing the Good News of our Savior. And it is important to remember that we bear testimony through both words and actions.

If you seek to be a radical follower of Christ, then it's time for you to share your testimony with others. So today, preach the Gospel through your words and your deeds . . . but not necessarily in that order.

To take up the cross means that you take your stand for the Lord Jesus no matter what it costs.

Billy Graham

Usually it is those who know Him that bring Him to others. That is why the Church, the whole body of Christians showing Him to one another, is so important.

C. S. Lewis

TODAY'S PRAYER

Lord, the life that I live and the words that I speak will tell the world how I feel about You. Today and every day, let my testimony be worthy of You. Let my words be sure and true, and let my actions point others to You. Amen

THE ULTIMATE CHOICE

For God so loved the world that He gave
His only begotten Son, that whoever believes in Him
should not perish but have everlasting life.

John 3:16 NKJV

Your ability to envision the future, like your life here on earth, is limited. God's vision, however, is not burdened by any such limitations. He sees all things, He knows all things, and His plans for you extend throughout eternity.

God's plans are not limited to the events of daily life. Your Heavenly Father has bigger things in mind for you . . . much bigger things. So praise the Creator for the gift of eternal life and share the Good News with all who cross your path. And remember: if you have given your heart to the Son, you belong to the Father—today, tomorrow, and for all eternity.

If you are a believer, your judgment will not determine your eternal destiny. Christ's finished work on Calvary was applied to you the moment you accepted Christ as Savior.

Beth Moore

Those of us who know the wonderful grace of redemption look forward to an eternity with God, when all things will be made new, when all our longings will at last find ultimate and final satisfaction.

Joseph Stowell

TODAY'S PRAYER

Lord, You have given me the priceless gift of eternal life through Your Son Jesus. Keep the hope of heaven fresh in my heart. While I am in this world, help me to pass through it with faith in my heart and praise on my lips for You. Amen

FOR I HAVE GIVEN YOU AN EXAMPLE THAT YOU ALSO SHOULD DO JUST AS I HAVE DONE FOR YOU.

—

John 13:15 HCSB